Standards and Assessment for Academic Libraries:

A Workbook

William Neal Nelson
Augusta State University

Robert W. Fernekes
Georgia Southern University

© 2002 ACRL, a division of American Library Association
Chicago, 2002

The paper used in this publication meets the minimum requirements of American National Standard for Information Sciences–Permanence of Paper for Printed Library Materials, ANSI Z39.48-1992. ∞

Library of Congress Cataloging-in-Publication Data
Nelson, William Neal, 1941-
   Standards and assessment for academic libraries : a workbook / William Neal Nelson, Robert W. Fernekes.
       p. cm.
Includes bibliographical references.
   ISBN 0-8389-8211-5 (alk. paper)
   1. Academic libraries--Standards--United States. 2. Academic libraries--United States--Evaluation. 3. Academic libraries--United States--Administration. I. Fernekes, Robert W. II. Association of College and Research Libraries. III. Title.

Z675.U5 N375 2002
027.7'0973--dc21

                      2002013786

Printed on recycled paper.

Printed in the United States of America.

06 05 04 03 02   5 4 3 2 1

Foreword

This workbook is designed to be used by academic libraries of all sizes, both public and private. It can be used to evaluate the academic library, and provides questions, worksheets, and suggested resources and sources of comparative data for this purpose. The workbook is the result of requests by librarians for a **practical** application of academic library standards.

The 2000 edition of the ACRL College Library Standards is used as a **framework** for the workbook; practical examples and applications from these standards are used because it is the first set of ACRL standards to incorporate outcomes assessment, as mandated by the ACRL Board in 1998. The CJCLS and ULS sections are also drafting such standards, and there is an attempt underway to develop a common set of ACRL standards. Until such common academic library standards are developed, the CLS standards can be used by all academic libraries implementing outcomes assessment.

The authors have worked with the current edition of the CLS standards since the draft stage and have become intimately familiar with the final product. As a member of the CLS Standards Committee that drafted the 2000 edition, Bob was a primary contributor of key sections, and reviewer of the entire document. As chair and member of the current CLS Standards Committee, Bill and Bob made several presentations designed to introduce the new edition of the standards to academic librarians. Widespread interest was immediately apparent and they were invited to make numerous additional presentations. The authors developed a presentation which evolved into a seminar/workshop with accompanying workbook–to date they have presented over a dozen workshops, from Albuquerque to Philadelphia and New Orleans to Davenport, Iowa.

Bill and Bob gratefully acknowledge the contributions of the librarians at Reese Library of Augusta State University for the development of several documents used in this workbook–special thanks go to Roxann Bustos, Associate Library Director, for her leadership in that effort. The authors are grateful to the many seminar/workshop participants who have provided frank and useful comments and suggestions on earlier versions of this workbook. They wish to thank those participants for improvements which have been incorporated into the present workbook, however, the authors accept responsibility for any errors and omissions. The workbook is under continuous revision—this version incorporates the current data available at the time of publication. Users are encouraged to provide suggestions for improvement to the authors, either directly or via ACRL.

Bob Fernekes
(fernekes@gasou.edu)

Bill Nelson
(wnelson@aug.edu)

Table of Contents

Regional Accrediting Association Standards: Links to CLS Standards

Introduction/Preface

Even though the newest Association of College and Research Libraries (ACRL) standards are for COLLEGE libraries, they are relevant to all academic libraries. Foremost, these standards incorporate **outcomes assessment** as defined by the ACRL Task Force Report on Academic Library Outcomes Assessment. Representing a departure from earlier ACRL standards, these are the first standards in the community college–college–university series to be outcomes-based.

The ACRL Board of Directors has mandated that all new and revised standards incorporate outcomes assessment, thus the newest Standards for College Libraries are serving as a model for applying outcomes assessment in these other standards. Recently, the University Libraries Section (ULS) Standards Committee chair invited the chairs of the assessment committees of the other two sections (CLS and CJCLS) to work together on a common set of standards for academic libraries. In 2002 the ACRL Board decided to appoint a College and Research Libraries Standards Task Force to facilitate this process and to make recommendations for implementation. We hope such an agreement becomes a reality in the not too distant future.

In any event, all institutions accredited by a regional accreditation agency and professional groups that expect outcomes assessment will gain valuable information and suggestions by reviewing these new standards. We encourage you to share these standards for use in your organization and by colleagues. They are available at http://www.ala.org/acrl/guides/college.html.

The goal of this workbook is to provide the user with:
1. A knowledge of the principles of the newest ACRL standards,
2. Worksheets to assist in the assessment process,
3. Practical examples to use as a guide to assessment techniques, and
4. Checklists and suggestions for application of these principles and practices to their own particular library.

For each of the 12 sections of the CLS standards, a matrix or chart with three columns is provided. Each chart includes selections from the CLS standards in the first column. The authors have identified performance areas and selected measures for demonstrating compliance (second column), and have provided suggested sources for assessment data and applications (third column). In addition, each section includes a methodology (including checklists and tips) for responding to evaluation questions.

Citations for the six regional accrediting association standards are provided at the end of the workbook, along with current status of each set of standards and the URLs of their webpages.

The following Appendices are included:

Appendix A - An annotated bibliography for additional background and information on academic library assessment.

Appendix B - A concept map that provides a graphic overview of the *Standards* and the relationship of the different functions, processes, outcomes performance indicators, and service quality dimensions. The graphic demonstrates the essential relationships among the institution mission, the library, and the user. The concept map provides a flow chart overview of these relationships. Traditional input and output examples are depicted above the flow chart. Aligned under institution mission are the uses of evaluation, assessment, and outcomes assessment. Likewise, aligned under the user are outcome performance indicators and service quality dimensions. The processes supporting the nine library functions listed in the concept map are examined in detail in the respective sections of the workbook.

Appendix C - A student satisfaction survey designed to collect data specifically for the sample evaluation plan provided.

Appendices D through I - A series of charts, one for each current and approved new standard, of all six of the regional accreditation associations. The charts depict a cross-reference between the individual sections of the *College Library Standards, 2000 Edition* and the regional accreditation association standards. The authors have examined the standards of the six regional accrediting associations and identified the requirements that can be linked to each of the 12 sections of the CLS Standards. These links for the current and new regional standards are presented in matrix form.

Part I: Overview
Planning, Assessment, and Outcomes Assessment

Introduction

These three sections are treated together in the *Standards*. For the workbook they are first discussed separately. Afterwards they are then treated as a group. A thorough understanding of this group is foundational for understanding the application of the other nine sections.

Chapter Organization and Description

Because of the close inter-relationships among planning, assessment, and outcomes assessment they are discussed in a manner different from the other nine sections.

Each chapter begins with a 3-column matrix to depict the relationship among library principles, performance areas, and data sources. Key principles promulgated in the *Standards* (column 1) provide the framework for identifying corresponding and related performance areas (column 2) coupled to their data sources, tools and suggested points of comparison (column 3). Essential ideas for each of these three sections are highlighted with excerpts from the *Standards*.

For **Planning** there is a discussion of the use of mission statements, with an example of an institutional and a library mission statement that is linked to it. Assessment bodies usually require that the two statements be linked; a simple method of demonstrating this linkage is provided.

For **Assessment** the construction and use of a planning matrix is discussed. A sample planning matrix is supplied along with a blank workform for use in completion of a plan by the user. A series of worksheets is provided with potential sources of data for assessment. Covered are: formal evaluation tools, using existing institutional evidence, and using statistical data for peer comparison.

In the **Outcomes Assessment** section, there is a discussion of "closing the assessment loop." First one must begin with an evaluation plan, then implement the evaluation procedures, and finally use the results. The ideal is to use the results for improvement. An actual example of this procedure is provided in the form of a long excerpt from a sample document, which also provides some practical examples to the user.

To draw together planning, assessment, and outcomes assessment a list of questions from the *Standards* is provided with some suggestions for a response. In conclusion there is a discussion of continuous improvement and a delineation of the steps necessary for closing the assessment loop.

ACRL Standards For College Libraries

(2000 Edition) http://www.ala.org/acrl/guides/college.html

The **Foreword** includes the following important definitions:

Inputs are generally regarded as the raw materials of a library program—the money, space, collection, equipment, and staff, out of which a program can arise.

Outputs serve to quantify the work done, i.e., number of books circulated, number of reference questions answered.

Outcomes are the ways in which library users are changed as a result of their contact with the library's resources and programs.

Points of Comparison is not a separate section, but can be used in a number of sections: Each college library is encouraged to choose its own peer group for the purpose of comparisons. Peer colleges may already be identified for benchmarking purposes by the college. If not, a peer group could be identified using criteria such as college mission, reputation, selectivity for admission, size of budget, size of endowment, expenditure for library support, and/or size of collection. Once a peer group has been determined, "points of comparison" can be made to compare the strength of the library with its peers. Suggested points of comparison for input and output measures are provided. This list is not to be considered exhaustive—other points of comparison can be determined by the college.

Planning, Assessment, and Outcomes Assessment
These 3 elements are the framework for the other 9 sections of the Standards.

Planning
The library should have a mission statement and goals to serve as a framework for its activities. The mission and goals should be compatible and consistent with those developed by the college. Assessment of the quality and effectiveness of the library should be linked closely with the specific mission and goals of the college. In order to build its programs and services in the context of the college, the library should be involved in the overall planning process. Formal planning procedures and methods, such as strategic planning, are used frequently. These planning methods require input from a broad spectrum of the college community. They help the college prepare for the future by clearly defining a vision and mission, by setting goals and objectives, and by implementing specific strategies or courses of action designed to help meet those ends. Strategic planning is an iterative process that includes evaluation, updating, and refinement. This process helps the college community focus on its essential values and provides an overall direction that helps to guide day-to-day activities and decisions.

Assessment [excerpt]

Comprehensive assessment requires the involvement of all categories of library users. The choice of clientele to be surveyed and questions to be asked should be made by the administration and the staff of the library with the assistance of an appropriate advisory committee. Questions should relate to how well the library supports its mission and how well it achieves its goals and objectives. Library users should be encouraged to offer signed or anonymous comments and suggestions. Opportunities for making suggestions should be available both in the library and through remote electronic access. All categories of users should be given an opportunity to participate in the evaluation. The weight given to responses should be consistent with the focus and mission of the library. A program of assessment and evaluation should take into consideration the changing rhythm of the academic year. Evaluation, whether it involves some or all of the techniques listed below, should be an ongoing process.

Outcomes Assessment

Outcomes assessment will increasingly measure and affect how library goals and objectives are achieved. It will address the accountability of institutions of higher education for student achievement and cost effectiveness. It should take into consideration libraries' greater dependence on technology, their increasing use of online services, their growing responsibility to provide information literacy skills, their increasing reliance on consortial services, the possibilities of dwindling financial resources for collection development, and new developments in the ways in which scholarly information is published and distributed.

Outcomes assessment can be an active mechanism for improving current library practices. It focuses on the achievement of outcomes that have been identified as desirable in the library's goals and objectives. It identifies performance measures, such as proficiencies, that indicate how well the library is doing what it has stated it wishes to do. Assessment instruments may include surveys, tests, interviews, and other valid measuring devices. These instruments may be specially designed for the function being measured, or previously developed instruments may be used. It is critical, however, to choose the instrument, the size of the sample, and the method used for sampling carefully. The instrument should be valid, and the way it is used should be appropriate for the task. Colleagues at peer institutions may render invaluable assistance by suggesting assessment questions and sample sizes, by sharing lessons learned, and suggesting alternative methods for measuring outcomes.

Other sections included in these Standards:

Services	Access	Communication and Cooperation
Instruction	Staff	Administration
Resources	Facilities	Budget

Chapter 1
PLANNING

Contents:

➢ Performance chart
➢ Use of Mission Statements in Planning and Assessment
➢ Library Mission Statement - Example
➢ Institutional Mission Statement - Example

Key Themes:

➢ Planning for library services is a continuing process.

➢ Assessment of library planning begins with a review of the library and institution missions and goals.

➢ Link the library's mission to the institutional mission.

➢ Demonstrate the linkage of the mission statements.

PLANNING

ACRL/CLS, *Standards 2000* (Excerpt)	Performance Areas & Selected Measures	Data Sources & Applications
• The library should have a **mission statement** and **goals** as the basis for its actions.	• Develop or review library **mission statement** with input from: ➤ library staff ➤ classroom faculty ➤ students ➤ administrators • Develop or review library **goals** (as above)	• Obtain information from the following: ➤ Institutional mission statement ➤ Library mission statement
• The library mission and goals should be compatible and <u>consistent with that of the institution.</u>	• Planning document identifies key institutional **outcomes** and **outputs** to which the library contributes. ➤ Review institutional documents	• Institutional planning documents • Academic unit planning documents • Academic support unit planning documents
• Assessment of library quality and effectiveness should be **linked closely** with specific mission and goals of the institution.	• Identify corresponding indicators whose measures document progress toward the realization of valued, campus-wide outcomes: ➤ student learning ➤ teaching ➤ scholarly activity	• Identify assessment measures and tools contained or referenced in above documents. ***Essential Ideas for PLANNING (See "Planning," p. 3)***

Excerpts in the above chart were taken from the following source: Column 1: "Standards for College Libraries, The Final Version, approved January 2000," *C&RL News,* March 2000, 61: 175-82. The intent of citing selected information is to display the inter-relationship of this document, and measures one can use to demonstrate continuing improvement. Material in Columns 2 and 3 was contributed by the authors.

Use of Mission Statements in Planning and Assessment

The following mission statements are provided as examples. They are used throughout this section to provide practical examples of the connections among planning, assessment, and outcomes assessment.

Academic library assessment and evaluation must begin with the institutional mission. The library mission must be consistent with the institutional mission. The examples provided demonstrate this inter-relationship.

The authors do not represent these as the best examples, or model statements. However, these examples from one institution are provided in order to give a practical example from a set of actual documents.

Reese Library Mission Statement

Reese Library supports the University curriculum by providing convenient, effective access to books and other information resources both locally and worldwide. In addition to maintaining a broad range of quality learning resources and services, the library stimulates teaching and learning by creating an environment in which instruction and research can flourish. In cooperation with other campus units, the library promotes the use of electronic information and instructional technologies and empowers its users with the information and technological competencies necessary to pursue their educational, research, and professional goals. Besides providing service to a diverse campus population, Reese Library serves as a cultural and intellectual resource for the local community, encouraging lifelong learning.

Placed in effect March 1, 1999. If you have any comments or suggestions toward our new statement, please contact our library director.

Available online at http://www.aug.edu/library/mission.html

Reese Library Mission Statement

<u>*Reese Library supports the University curriculum* by *providing convenient, effective access to books and other information resources both locally and worldwide*</u>. In addition to <u>*maintaining a broad range of quality learning resources and services,*</u> the library <u>*stimulates teaching and learning by creating an environment in which instruction and research can flourish*</u>. In <u>*cooperation with other campus units,*</u> the library <u>*promotes the use of electronic information and instructional technologies*</u> and <u>*empowers its users with the information and technological competencies necessary to pursue their educational, research, and professional goals.*</u> Besides providing <u>*service to a diverse campus population*</u>, Reese Library <u>*serves as a cultural and intellectual resource for the local community, encouraging lifelong learning.*</u>

Effective date: March 1, 1999

Entries in *italics*/<u>**underlined**</u> are taken directly from this Reese Library Mission Statement and included in the "Purpose" and "Goals" columns of the Reese Library Evaluation Plan (See chart beginning on page 15).

AUGUSTA STATE UNIVERSITY
Mission Statement

Augusta State University is committed to **excellence in teaching, advancement of knowledge, and enrichment of the community** in a climate that fosters humane values and a **life-long love of learning**. With origins in the founding of the Academy of Richmond County in 1783 and the creation of a separate Junior College of Augusta in 1925, its mission is predicated on the cultural, social, and economic value of a strong liberal arts education. This **enlarges its students' individual** versatility, creative powers, cultural appreciation, knowledge of the world, respect for others, and **professional expertise**.

Augusta State University strives to be a national model of excellence for its **quality of service** to the second largest metropolitan area in Georgia. With a broad array of undergraduate programs and a select offering of graduate programs below the doctoral level, it functions as a metropolitan, non-residential university for the area.

Open to the voices of all its members, the university **serves a population diverse in race, background, age, and preparation**. It provides access not only to those who are fully ready for college but also to the underprepared who show potential and to those seeking the kind of academic challenge normally associated with elite, private institutions.

Emphasizing student-faculty contact, the university **fosters intellectual growth** through learning assistance, honors courses, and **student research**. It **promotes electronic information technologies** and **links students with the world community of scholarship**.

The university **collaborates with the Medical College of Georgia, Paine College, Augusta Technical Institute**, Fort Gordon, and P-12 schools. It makes constant, programmatic use of local industries, agencies, and institutions as laboratories for practical learning experiences. In an area with a large health care industry, it provides undergraduate general education courses for the Medical College students, prepares students to enter programs at that institution, and educates others to work in the medical field. It is also the principal source of training for the area's teachers and business leaders.

Augusta State University is acutely conscious of its **responsibility to a community** where its graduates become teachers and artists, professionals and civic leaders. It **seeks to serve: enriching its area culturally**, improving economic and social conditions, and **promoting personal and professional development**. To these ends, the university cultivates intellectually vital faculty members who are excellent in teaching, active in research, generous in service, and committed to its mission. The university also strives to have its faculty, staff, curriculum, and **programs reflect the increasing diversity of the population** and world from which its students come.

Devoted to constant improvement, the university assesses its performance by evaluating its stewardship of resources, responsiveness to area needs, involvement with its community, the response of the public it serves, and, most importantly, the success of the students it educates.

NOTE: *Entries <u>underlined</u> reflect direct connections from this University Mission Statement to the Reese Library Mission, and are included in the "Purpose" and "Goals" columns of the Matrix.* **Available online at http://www.aug.edu/mission.html**

Chapter 2

ASSESSMENT

Contents:

- ➤ Performance chart
- ➤ Use of a Planning Matrix in Library Assessment
- ➤ Library Purposes and Goals - Example
- ➤ Library Evaluation Plan - Example of an Assessment Planning Matrix
- ➤ Worksheet for Assessment
- ➤ Worksheet for Identifying Existing Institutional Evidence
- ➤ Worksheet for Identifying Statistical Data for Peer Comparison
- ➤ Worksheet for Developing a Library Planning Chart

Key Themes:

- ➤ Assessment should explore how well the library supports its mission and how well it achieves its goals and objectives.

- ➤ Library assessment is a continuing process using a variety of methods to evaluate the following performance areas:
  - *Services*
  - *Instruction*
  - *Resources*
  - *Access*
  - *Staff*
  - *Facilities*
  - *Budget*

- ➤ Existing library and institutional data can be used in the assessment process.

- ➤ A planning matrix can be a useful tool for library assessment, as it can:
  - *Provide a graphic display of assessment elements.*
  - *Show the interrelationship among the assessment elements and processes.*
  - *Display proposed evaluation procedures and planned use of results.*

ASSESSMENT

ACRL/CLS, *Standards* 2000 (Excerpt)	Performance Areas [For Selected Measures, see the individual section matrix]	Data Sources & Applications
• **Comprehensive assessment** requires the involvement of all categories of library users plus non-users. • Questions should relate to **how well** the library supports its mission and **how well** it achieves its goals and objectives.	• **Services**–provide a range of quality services; prompt & competent assistance to users; reasonable & convenient hours; reference assistance; availability to off-campus programs and users • **Instruction**–provide a variety of formal & informal instruction in use of library materials in all formats; integrate information literacy skills into instruction. • **Resources**–provide varied, authoritative, and up-to-date resources in a variety of formats; maintain currency by weeding • **Access**–provided in a timely & orderly fashion; maintain a central catalog of library resources; support distance learners with equivalent means of access. • **Staff**–of sufficient size & quantity to meet programmatic & service needs of primary users; well-qualified & trained • **Facilities**–well-planned, secure, adequate space; conducive to study and research; climate-controlled environment • **Budget**–meet reasonable expectations of users; support appropriate levels of staffing; support adequate collection	• Examples of quantitative and qualitative data the library collects about its performance and uses to assess itself: ➢ Surveys — General library knowledge — Graduating student — Focus groups ➢ Internal evaluations ➢ Outside evaluators ➢ Pre- and Post-tests to measure results of library instruction. ➢ Recommendations by regional and specialized accrediting agencies, such as: — NCATE — AACSB — NASM — NLN • Relevant data collected from all sources is compiled & summarized in a planning matrix or chart. *NOTE: for more specific DATA SOURCES, see each individual section matrix. Essential Ideas for ASSESSMENT (See "Assessment," p. 4)*
See page 6 for complete citations.		

Use of a Planning Matrix

For a graphic display of the library assessment process, a planning matrix or chart can be used. The sample library mission is presented here in outline form.

The sample library planning matrix is formed by constructing four columns titled respectively, "Purpose," "Goal," "Evaluation Procedure," and "Use of Results." The information for the first two columns is entered from the library mission outline.

For each goal, multiple evaluation procedures are proposed and entered in column 3. For each evaluation procedure, a proposed use of results is entered in column 4. As a last step, the frequency of the evaluation procedure is projected; in the example a code is entered into the third column for this purpose.

To assist in identifying assessment procedures, some formal evaluation tools are listed. Also provided are examples of some existing institutional evidence that can be used, and some sources of statistical data for peer comparison.

A blank workform is provided for entry of the data to draft a planning matrix for your own library.

Reese Library Purposes/ Goals - Outline
September 1999

Outline format:
I. Purpose
    A. Goal

Entries in ***italics and bold*** are taken directly from the Reese Library Mission Statement, approved on March 1, 1999 and included in the library Web pages.
Entries <u>underlined</u> reflect direct connections with the University Mission Statement.

I. Reese Library will support the University curriculum.
    A. <u>*Provide convenient, effective access to books and other information resources both locally and worldwide*</u>
    B. *Maintain a broad range of <u>quality learning resources and services</u>*
    C. <u>*Promote the use of electronic information and instructional technologies*</u>
    D. Cooperate with state, regional, and national library-service providers to expeditiously deliver materials and information

II. Reese Library will <u>stimulate teaching and learning</u>.
    A. *Create an environment in which <u>instruction and research can flourish</u>*
    B. *Empower users with the <u>information and technological competencies necessary to pursue their educational, research, and professional goals</u>*
    C. <u>Foster student research through faculty-student contact</u>, using library instruction
    D. *Cooperate with other campus units*
    E. <u>Cooperate with local public and academic libraries in serving the campus community</u>

III. Reese Library will <u>serve a diverse campus population</u>.
    A. Provide an effective collection
    B. Provide effective library services
    C. Provide an effective staff
    D. Provide effective equipment
    E. Provide occasional library <u>cultural events</u>

IV. Reese Library will serve as a <u>cultural and intellectual resource for the local community</u>.
    A. <u>*Encourage lifelong learning*</u>
    B. <u>Provide community access</u> to print and electronic materials
    C. <u>Provide community access</u> to Georgia and federal government documents
    D. <u>Ensure the local community is invited to library cultural events</u>

REESE LIBRARY EVALUATION PLAN
(Planning Matrix Completed)

Purpose	Goal	Evaluation Procedure*	Use of Results
I. Reese Library will support the University curriculum	A. Provide convenient, effective access to books and other information resources both locally and worldwide	1. Conduct regular surveys to assess the effectiveness of the online library catalog in allowing users to find their resources[3]	Review results to determine whether users are satisfied with the OPAC, and take appropriate action based on results
		2. Calculate ratio of ILL materials requested to those delivered[1]	Analyze results; determine reasons for non-delivery and adjust procedures, as appropriate
		3. Analyze GALILEO statistics to determine usage by ASU community and compare to peer libraries[1]	If usage significantly differs from peers, determine the reasons and adjust procedures, as appropriate
	B. Maintain a broad range of quality learning resources and services	1. Periodically survey users to assess effectiveness of resources and services in meeting their research needs[2]	Analyze results; seek appropriate ways to meet identified needs
		2. Survey student library users regarding library materials for their major[C]	Analyze data and take appropriate action
		3. Survey faculty regarding library material for their courses[2]	Analyze data and take appropriate action
	C. Promote the use of electronic information and instructional technologies	1. Monitor attendance each semester at drop-in instructional sessions emphasizing the use of electronic information and/or instructional technologies[S]	Improve publicity or adjust number of sessions as needed based on high or low attendance

*Frequency of Evaluation
KEY: 1 = Annually; 2 = Every 2 years; 3 = Every 3 years; C = Continuous or Ongoing; S = Twice a year (fall & spring semester)

REESE LIBRARY EVALUATION PLAN
(Planning Matrix Completed)

Purpose	Goal	Evaluation Procedure*	Use of Results
		2. Determine ratio of students participating in library instruction sessions to total student population[S]	Analyze trend and make adjustments as necessary
		3. Conduct faculty and staff training sessions in use of electronic information and instructional technologies[C]	Evaluate results of training and cooperate with Training Triad to improve instruction
	D. Cooperate with state, regional, and national library-service providers to expeditiously deliver materials and information	1. Review contracts and cooperative agreements annually[1]	Revise as necessary
		2. Calculate ILL delivery time[1]	Analyze results; take appropriate action
		3. Review GALILEO usage statistics[1]	Take appropriate action
		4. Review GIL usage statistics[1]	Analyze results; take appropriate action
	A. Create an environment in which instruction and research can flourish	1. Conduct a library satisfaction survey[3]	Identify problem areas and seek explanations/solutions
II. Reese Library will stimulate teaching and learning.		2. Compare staff, space, and funding to specifications in the College Library Standards (1995)[3]	a. Review grades of C and below to determine specific problems—seek more detail, as needed and seek resources necessary to improve verified deficiencies and/or problems b. Review grades of "B" and above to determine points of excellence

*Frequency of Evaluation
KEY: 1 = Annually; 2 = Every 2 years; 3 = Every 3 years; C = Continuous or Ongoing; S = Twice a year (fall & spring semester)

Standards and Assessment for Academic Libraries: A Workbook

REESE LIBRARY EVALUATION PLAN
(Planning Matrix Completed)

Purpose	Goal	Evaluation Procedure*	Use of Results
		3. Assess outcomes assessment measures recommended in the new DRAFT College Library Standards (July 1999)[1]	Include appropriate outcomes assessment measures in ongoing collection, evaluation, and planning activities
	B. Empower users with the information and technological competencies necessary to pursue their educational, research, and professional goals	1. Measure results of library instruction by pre- and post-tests of students[C]	Identify and correct areas of weakness and reinforce areas of strength
		2. Survey faculty on the value of library instruction for improvement of their students' research skills[S]	Analyze results; determine why evaluation of improvement is below are above goal
	C. Foster student research through faculty-student contact, using library instruction	1. Measure results of library instruction by pre- and post-tests of students[C]	Identify and correct areas of weakness and reinforce areas of strength in research strategies
		2. Survey faculty on the value of library instruction for improvement of their students' research skills[2]	Analyze results; work with classroom faculty to determine areas for improvement
		3. Survey students on the value of library instruction for improvement of their information literacy & technology skills[1]	Analyze results; determine why evaluation of improvement is below are above goal
	D. Cooperate with other campus units	1. Periodically review information concerning library assistance provided to campus units[S]	Modify procedures/methods as necessary

*Frequency of Evaluation
KEY: 1 = Annually; 2 = Every 2 years; 3 = Every 3 years; C = Continuous or Ongoing; S = Twice a year (fall & spring semester)

REESE LIBRARY EVALUATION PLAN
(Planning Matrix Completed)

Purpose	Goal	Evaluation Procedure*	Use of Results
	E. Cooperate with local public and academic libraries in serving the campus community	1. Review cooperative agreements[1]	Revise as necessary
III. Reese Library will serve a diverse campus population.	A. Provide an effective collection	1. Survey all segments of the user population to determine satisfaction with the collection[3]	Analyze results and modify Collection Development Policy and procedures as necessary
		2. Compare segments of the collection to standard bibliographies and peer library collections[1]	Identify strengths and weaknesses; take necessary and appropriate action
		3. Examine segments of the collection for relevancy and currency of materials[C]	In consultation with classroom faculty, remove irrelevant and dated materials
	B. Provide effective library services	1. Assess library services by surveys, with input from all segments of the campus population[3]	Identify unserved/underserved segments and develop a strategy to ensure they are appropriately served
	C. Provide an effective staff	1. Employ regular library user satisfaction surveys, specifically inquiring about staff performance[3]	Conduct regular workshops for library staff in areas of users' concerns
		2. Survey staff to identify areas of need for staff development and training[1]	a. Provide appropriate and varied opportunities for needed staff development b. Provide necessary staff training

*Frequency of Evaluation
KEY: 1 = Annually; 2 = Every 2 years; 3 = Every 3 years; C = Continuous or Ongoing; S = Twice a year (fall & spring semester)

REESE LIBRARY EVALUATION PLAN
(Planning Matrix Completed)

Purpose	Goal	Evaluation Procedure*	Use of Results
		3. Review advertised opportunities for staff and faculty development and training[C]	Select appropriate development and training opportunities for staff and faculty
		4. Review all job descriptions[1]	Modify job descriptions as appropriate
	D. Provide effective equipment	1. Assess use of current equipment[1]	Repair and upgrade equipment as necessary and appropriate
		2. Conduct periodic surveys to determine whether equipment meets research needs[3]	a. Analyze results to determine needs b. Correct any deficiencies and/or problems noted by users with respect to disabilities or level of abilities
	E. To provide periodic library cultural events	1. Survey campus community to determine satisfaction with library-sponsored events and solicit recommendations[3]	Analyze results; take appropriate action
IV. Reese Library will serve as a cultural and intellectual resource for the local community.	A. Encourage lifelong learning	1. Assess library success in preparing graduates for lifelong learning with questions included on the graduating student and alumni surveys[1]	Based on results, modify library programs, as appropriate
	B. Provide community access to print and electronic materials	1. Track the number of Community User cards issued and analyze numbers to measure increased or decreased use of the print collection[1]	Analyze results and modify Community User procedures as necessary and appropriate

*Frequency of Evaluation
KEY: 1 = Annually; 2 = Every 2 years; 3 = Every 3 years; C = Continuous or Ongoing; S = Twice a year (fall & spring semester)

REESE LIBRARY EVALUATION PLAN
(Planning Matrix Completed)

Purpose	Goal	Evaluation Procedure*	Use of Results
		2. Analyze requests of material from community users via request cards, suggestion boxes and the library web page to determine local community needs[C]	Order requested items as necessary and appropriate
		3. Assess the Browsing Collection through surveys and suggestion box input to determine user satisfaction[3]	Adjust selection of Browsing books as necessary
	C. Provide community access to Georgia and federal government documents	1. Review latest GPO and Library evaluations of the documents operation[3]	Adjust selection as necessary and appropriate
		2. Review the government documents collection for deselection of unnecessary materials[C]	Deselect and dispose of unnecessary materials in order to increase the percentage of useful and needed materials.
		3. Survey library users to determine whether GALILEO provides adequate access to Georgia documents[3]	Modify provision of Georgia documents as appropriate and feasible
	D. Ensure the local community is invited to library cultural events	1. Assess effectiveness of promotional efforts[C]	Modify efforts as appropriate

*Frequency of Evaluation
KEY: 1 = Annually; 2 = Every 2 years; 3 = Every 3 years; C = Continuous or Ongoing; S = Twice a year (fall & spring semester)

NOTE: "Evaluation Schedule for Reese Library," provides specific dates for evaluation of goals.

© 1999, Reese Library, Augusta State University
Questions should be directed to Bill Nelson (wnelson@aug.edu) or Roxann Bustos (rbustos@aug.edu)

Assessment Worksheet

Formal evaluation tools may include the following:

General library knowledge surveys (or "pre-tests") offered to incoming first year students, re-offered at a mid-point in the students' careers and again near graduation, to assess whether the library's program of curricular instruction is producing more information-literate students. *(List those currently used or proposed.)*

Evaluation checklists for librarian and tutorial instruction to gather feedback from students, other librarians and teaching faculty. *(List those currently used or proposed.)*

Student journal entries, or information literacy diaries, used to track their library use. *(List those currently used or proposed–identify class(es) or programs where produced.)*

Focus groups of students, faculty, staff, and alumni who are asked to comment on their experiences using information resources over a period of time. *(List those already conducted or proposed.)*

Assessment and evaluation by librarians from other colleges and/or other appropriate consultants. *(List those already conducted or proposed.)*

Reviews of specific library and information service areas and/or operations. *(List those currently used or proposed–indicate sponsor, i.e. Library, VPAA, etc.)*

Identifying Existing Institutional Evidence– Worksheet

(assessments, reports, surveys, etc.)

Examples:
  ➢ Institutional Self-Studies for regional and specialized accreditation agencies such as Southern Association of Colleges and Schools (SACS), National Council for Accreditation of Teacher Education (NCATE), etc.
  ➢ Visiting Committee Reports (SACS, NCATE, etc.)
  ➢ Library Annual Reports, Integrated Postsecondary Education Data System (IPEDS) survey, Academic Library Survey (ALS), etc.
  ➢ Surveys (User Satisfaction, Graduating Student, ACT Student Opinion, etc.)

List those currently available, or expected to be used.

1.

2.

3.

4.

5.

Standards and Assessment for Academic Libraries: A Workbook

Identifying Statistical Data For Peer Comparison–Worksheet

IPEDS/ ALS (data available from various sources)

—ALA web site for Academic Library Survey (http://www.ala.org/alaorg/ors/ncesals.html)

• Summary of Academic Library Survey (http://nces.ed.gov/surveys/libraries/academic.asp)

• 1998 data (released in July 2002) available here

• Academic Library Peer Comparison Tool, for 1998 ALS data

Peer Academic Library Statistics (PALS) – IPEDS data available from John Minter Associates (http://www.jma-inc.net/about.shtml)

ACRL Data Survey (print available from ACRL)

—1997–98 **electronic version** commercially available through SCHOLARSTAT

—1998–99 **electronic version** available from ACRL (http://acrl.telusys.net/trendstat/index.html)

* Data from 1,367 academic libraries in all Carnegie classifications is included.

* Also included is data on faculty status for academic librarians.

—1999–2000 **electronic version** available from ACRL (http://acrl.telusys.net/trendstat/2000/)

* Data from 1,678 academic libraries in all Carnegie classifications is included.

* Also included is data on institutions' activities in providing library services for distance learning.

• 1998 Statistical Summaries (http://fisher.lib.virginia.edu/acrl/1998/index.html)

• 1999 Statistical Summaries (http://fisher.lib.virginia.edu/acrl/1999/)

ARL Statistics (http://www.arl.org/stats/arlstat/)

—1999–2000 is latest available data (published annually since 1908)

List those your library can expect to use.

1.

2.

3.

4.

YOUR LIBRARY GOALS & EVALUATION PROCEDURES–WORKSHEET

2002-2003

Purpose	Goal	Evaluation Procedure	Use of Results

YOUR LIBRARY GOALS & EVALUATION PROCEDURES–WORKSHEET

2002-2003

Purpose	Goal	Evaluation Procedure	Use of Results

Chapter 3
OUTCOMES ASSESSMENT

Contents:

 ➢ Performance chart
 ➢ Closing the Loop
 ➢ Reese Library Closing the Loop
 ➢ Planning, Assessment, & Outcomes Assessment
 ➢ Continuous Improvement: Closing the Assessment Loop

Key Themes:

 ➢ Outcomes assessment focuses on the achievement of outcomes that have been identified as desirable in the library's goals and objectives.
   • *Determine what outcomes are to be measured.*

 ➢ Outcomes assessment identifies performance measures that indicate how well the library is doing what it has stated it wishes to do.
   • *Select appropriate performance areas.*
   • *Determine appropriate evaluation measures for the selected performance areas.*

 ➢ Comprehensive assessment includes:
   • *Development of an evaluation plan*
   • *Implementation of an evaluation plan*
   • *Closing the loop by use of the assessment results.*
   • *Repetition of the process for continuous improvement.*

OUTCOMES ASSESSMENT

ACRL/CLS, *Standards 2000* (Excerpt)	Performance Areas & Selected Measures	Data Sources & Applications
• Outcomes assessment focuses on the **achievement of outcomes** that have been identified as desirable in the library's goals and objectives.	• Determine what outcomes are to be measured, such as student learning and program effectiveness, per the library assessment plan (derived from goals and objectives).	*Obtain information from the following:* ➢ *Institutional satisfaction surveys* *— student* *— faculty* *— graduating student* ➢ *Institutional self-study documents*
• Outcomes assessment identifies **performance measures** that indicate how well the library is doing what it has stated it wishes to do.	• Select appropriate performance areas from Section 2 (Assessment) that will be evaluated. • Determine appropriate evaluation measures to use for each of the selected performance areas **(see individual section matrices).** • Once data is collected and analyzed, it should be used, either for decision-making and/or as the basis for further analysis. **The ultimate goal is continuing improvement of library operations by assessing outcomes.** • Data is recorded and results used for improvement. Use of results is summarized in the planning chart or matrix, closing the assessment loop. • The assessment process continues, beginning with a review of the library mission and goals.	➢ *Regional and specialized accreditation committee reports* ➢ *Pre- and post-tests of students receiving library instruction* ➢ *Library annual reports* ➢ *Higher Education data* *— IPEDS/ALS (1998 available)* ➢ *National Data for Library Peer Comparison* *— Academic Library Survey* *— ACRL survey data (1998, 1999, & 2000 available)* *— ARL statistics (1908 –2000 available)* ***Essential Ideas for OUTCOMES ASSESSMENT (See "Outcomes Assessment," p. 4)***
See page 6 for complete citations.		

Closing the Loop

The evaluation plan is the first step in a comprehensive assessment. In order to complete the loop, the evaluation procedures must be implemented and the results used.

An actual example of this procedure is provided in the form of an excerpt of the complete document from the library used as an example.

This sample document includes ten years of historical material to show a progression of evaluation and how the results are used in a new evaluation procedure. It is not necessary to include material for such a long period of time, but it can prove useful for a summary of assessment and evaluation efforts since the last accreditation visit. For example, in IB of the sample (p. 30) a survey was conducted and it was used to produce a 1990 self-study report. This report led to an *institutional* self-study report, which in turn made four recommendations, which were implemented. That report was then reviewed by SACS (Commission on Colleges of the Southern Association of Colleges and Schools–the regional accrediting agency), which made a further recommendation leading to an institutional decision for charging the faculty Library Committee with conducting an annual evaluation of library services.

This sample document provides additional practical examples, some of which may be applied to other academic library situations.

Appendix C is an example of a student survey. This particular survey was designed to gather information specifically for the sample evaluation plan provided here.

Finally, a worksheet is provided to assist the library in outcomes assessment.

CLOSING THE LOOP
REESE LIBRARY GOALS AND EVALUATION PROCEDURES
(Excerpt)

Purpose	Goal	Evaluation Procedure*	Use of Results
I. Reese Library will support the University curriculum	A. Provide convenient, effective access to books and other information resources both locally and worldwide	1. Conduct regular surveys to determine the success of users in locating material in the catalog, in the library, and online a. 1990 Reese Library Survey b. 1991 SACS Report—RECOMMENDATION: Demonstrate regular & systematic evaluation of the library & its policies. c. Next–Conduct a Survey designed by Library Committee (Spring 2000)[3]	a. USE: 1990 Self-Study Report produced b. USE: ASU Library Committee will have annual assignment of evaluation of library to ensure it is serving the needs of its users. c. Next–Review results to determine whether users are satisfied with the tools & methods for locating materials, and take appropriate action based on results
		2. Calculate ratio of ILL materials requested to those delivered[1]	Analyze results; determine reasons for non-delivery and adjust procedures, as appropriate
		3. Analyze GALILEO statistics to determine usage by ASU community and compare to peer libraries a. Analyzed total GALILEO keyword searches (4 years) and compared with USG peer institutions[1]	If usage significantly differs from peers, determine the reasons and adjust procedures, as appropriate a. Analysis shows ASU usage numbers for GALILEO are comparable to 4 peers in the USG. Based on this evaluation, there is no reason to adjust procedures at this time.

*Frequency of Evaluation
KEY: 1 = Annually; 2 = Every 2 years; 3 = Every 3 years; C = Continuous or Ongoing; S = Twice a year (fall & spring semester)

CLOSING THE LOOP
REESE LIBRARY GOALS AND EVALUATION PROCEDURES
(Excerpt)

Purpose	Goal	Evaluation Procedure*	Use of Results
	B. Maintain a broad range of quality learning resources and services	1. Periodically survey users to assess effectiveness of resources and services in meeting their research needs a. 1990 Reese Library Survey (Satisfaction with library holdings) b. 1990 AC Self-Study Report–RECOMMENDATION: 1. Add current journal subscriptions, 2. Weed collection, 3. More microforms, 4. More electronic formats. c. 1991 SACS Report–RECOMMENDATION: Demonstrate regular & systematic evaluation of the library & its policies. d. 1994 Student Satisfaction Survey e. 1995 Student Profile (Adequacy of Library holdings) f. 1990-99 ACT Student Opinion Survey (Student satisfaction with library facilities & services) g. 1999 Graduating Student Survey (Student satisfaction: Library Services- overall; Library Collections- overall) h. 1999 Student Satisfaction Survey i. Next–Conduct a Survey designed by the Library Committee (Spr. 2000)[2]	a. USE: 1990 Self-Study Report produced b. USE: 1. $75,000 added to library budget, 1991-92 for current journals 2. 38,048 volumes weeded, 1991-92 3. Several major microform collections added 4. CD-ROM tower added, 1993; many other formats also added since then. In 1999 web-based products predominate, with 155 products available through GALILEO and by subscription. c. USE: ASU Library Committee will have annual assignment of evaluation of library to ensure it is serving the needs of its users. (Conducted survey, 1994. Designing survey, 2000.) *(continued on next page)*

(continued on next page)

*Frequency of Evaluation
KEY: 1 = Annually; 2 = Every 2 years; 3 = Every 3 years; C = Continuous or Ongoing; S = Twice a year (fall & spring semester)

CLOSING THE LOOP

REESE LIBRARY GOALS AND EVALUATION PROCEDURES

(Excerpt)

Purpose	Goal	Evaluation Procedure*	Use of Results
			d. USE: 1. Identified dissatisfaction with library hours-produced a Report on Reese Library Hours 2. Identified need for services-added photocopiers outside the library; added 24-hour computer lab outside the library. 3. Identified needs of night & nontraditional students-ASU formed Night & Non-traditional Student Advocacy Group, September1996 (Library Director appointed as an original member) e. Reviewed results: 58% rated holdings "good" or "excellent;" 10% rated them as "poor:" Some concern about results-no specifics identified. f. Reviewed results: consistently high satisfaction rating; last 5 years slightly higher satisfaction rating. No concerns identified g. Overall Library Services-93% satisfaction rating; Overall Library Collections-81% satisfaction rating. No concerns identified. h. Awaiting results i. Next–Analyze results; seek appropriate ways to meet identified needs

*Frequency of Evaluation

KEY: 1 = Annually; 2 = Every 2 years; 3 = Every 3 years; C = Continuous or Ongoing; S = Twice a year (fall & spring semester)

CLOSING THE LOOP
REESE LIBRARY GOALS AND EVALUATION PROCEDURES
(Excerpt)

Purpose	Goal	Evaluation Procedure*	Use of Results
		2. Survey student library users regarding library materials for their major a. 1990 Reese Library Survey (Satisfaction with library holdings) b. 1995 Student Profile (Adequacy of Library holdings) c. 1999 Graduating Student Survey d. Next–continue graduating student survey; incorporate appropriate question(s) into other surveys[c]	a. USE: 1990 Self-Study Report produced b. Only addressed adequacy of general collection, not specific majors c. Reviewed results: 81 percent satisfaction rating for "books/journals in my major;" less than 4% "very dissatisfied." No specific concerns identified–need further data d. Next–Analyze data and take appropriate action
		3. Survey faculty regarding library material for their courses a. 1999 Faculty Survey b. Next–Conduct a survey designed by the Library Committee (Spr. 2000)[2]	a. Reviewed results: some dissatisfaction with holdings, especially in Chemistry/ Physics, & Biology. Requesting additional funding for materials in FY2001 budget b. Next–Analyze data and take appropriate action
	C. Promote the use of electronic information and instructional technologies	1. Monitor attendance each semester at drop-in instructional sessions emphasizing the use of electronic information and/or instructional technologies[S]	Improve publicity or adjust number of sessions as needed based on high or low attendance
		2. Determine ratio of students participating in library instruction sessions to total student population a. 1990 Reese Library Survey b. Next–Calculate ratio[S]	a. USE: 1990 Self-Study Report produced b. Next–Analyze trend and make adjustments as necessary

*Frequency of Evaluation
KEY: 1 = Annually; 2 = Every 2 years; 3 = Every 3 years; C = Continuous or Ongoing; S = Twice a year (fall & spring semester)

Standards and Assessment for Academic Libraries: A Workbook

CLOSING THE LOOP
REESE LIBRARY GOALS AND EVALUATION PROCEDURES
(Excerpt)

Purpose	Goal	Evaluation Procedure*	Use of Results
		3. Conduct faculty and staff training sessions in use of electronic information and instructional technologies[C]	Evaluate results of training and cooperate with Training Triad to improve instruction
	D. Cooperate with state, regional, and national library-service providers to expeditiously deliver materials and information	1. Review contracts and cooperative agreements annually a. Review cost of OCLC dedicated line, and available options[1]	Revise as necessary. a. OCLC access changed from dedicated phone line to web-based access (January, 1999)
		2. Calculate ILL delivery time[1]	Analyze results; take appropriate action
		3. Review GALILEO usage statistics a. Analyzed ASU usage statistics for GALILEO since its inception[1]	Take appropriate action a. Expeditious delivery of information is available through GALILEO, and ASU users have taken advantage of it by executing almost 400,000 keyword searches since its inception.
		4. Review GIL usage statistics (Will begin after GIL implementation in June 2000)[1]	Analyze results; take appropriate action
II. Reese Library will stimulate teaching and learning.	A. Create an environment in which instruction and research can flourish	1. Conduct a library satisfaction survey a. 1990 Reese Library (Overall rating; library hours)	a. RESULT: New survey, with focus on library hours. USE: 1990 Self-Study Report produced
		(continued on next page)	*(continued on next page)*

*Frequency of Evaluation
KEY: 1 = Annually; 2 = Every 2 years; 3 = Every 3 years; C = Continuous or Ongoing; S = Twice a year (fall & spring semester)

CLOSING THE LOOP
REESE LIBRARY GOALS AND EVALUATION PROCEDURES
(Excerpt)

Purpose	Goal	Evaluation Procedure*	Use of Results
		e. 1990-99 ACT Student Opinion Survey (Student satisfaction with library facilities & services) f. 1997-98 USG Student Satisfaction Survey g. Conduct regular count of actual late-night users h. Compare ASU library hours with peer institutions i. Next-New Survey, under development by the Library Committee (Spring 2000)[3]	d. Reviewed results: 69% rated hours as "good" or "excellent;" fewer than 10% rated them as "poor" e. See IB1f f. Reviewed results: ASU satisfaction rating 3.94-compares favorably with 3.90 national, and 3.91 Georgia peer groups. No concerns noted. g. Night Count of Library Users shows a relatively small number of users after 9:30 p.m. This information shows no apparent need for extended hours. h. Comparison with peer institutions in the USG shows ASU library hours to be comparable. No apparent need identified for additional hours. i. Next-Identify problem areas and seek explanations/solutions

*Frequency of Evaluation
KEY: 1 = Annually; 2 = Every 2 years; 3 = Every 3 years; C = Continuous or Ongoing; S = Twice a year (fall & spring semester)

CLOSING THE LOOP
REESE LIBRARY GOALS AND EVALUATION PROCEDURES
(Excerpt)

Purpose	Goal	Evaluation Procedure*	Use of Results
		2. Compare staff, space, and funding to specifications in the College Library Standards (1995 edition) a. 1999 (1998 data) –Assessment of Reese Library conducted and a report produced[3]	• Review grades of C and below to determine specific problems—seek more detail, as needed and seek resources necessary to improve verified deficiencies/problems • Review grades of "B" and above to determine points of excellence a. Assessment Results: 1. Mission–compliance achieved 2. Collections (overall quantity)–grade is A+ 3. Organization of materials–compliance achieved 4. Staff– grade is D- 5. Services–compliance achieved 6. Facilities–grade is D 7. Administration–compliance achieved 8. Budget–needs improvement USE: Requested increase in staff, space & budget for FY2001.
		3. Assess outcomes assessment measures recommended in the new DRAFT College Library Standards (July 1999) a. Final standards approved, January 2000.[1]	Include appropriate outcomes assessment measures in ongoing collection, evaluation, and planning activities a. Presently under review by Reese Library staff

*Frequency of Evaluation
KEY: 1 = Annually; 2 = Every 2 years; 3 = Every 3 years; C = Continuous or Ongoing; S = Twice a year (fall & spring semester)

CLOSING THE LOOP
REESE LIBRARY GOALS AND EVALUATION PROCEDURES
(Excerpt)

Purpose	Goal	Evaluation Procedure*	Use of Results
	B. Empower users with the information and technological competencies necessary to pursue their educational, research, and professional goals	1. Measure results of library instruction by pre- and post-tests of students[c]	Identify and correct areas of weakness and reinforce areas of strength
		2. Survey faculty on the value of library instruction for improvement of their students' information literacy & technology skills a. Faculty evaluate library instruction sessions provided to their students (use web survey form) b. New Survey, under development by Library Committee (Spring 2000)[S]	a. Improvements in library instruction based on evaluations include: publishing library handouts on the webpage, and development and use of a library skills core list. b. Next–Analyze results; determine why evaluation of improvement is below are above goal
		3. Survey students on the value of library instruction for improvement of their information literacy & technology skills a. Students evaluate library instruction sessions they receive (can use hardcopy or web survey form) b. New Survey under development by Library Committee[1]	a. Improvements in library instruction based on evaluations include: publishing library handouts on the webpage, and development and use of a library skills core list. b. Next–Analyze results; determine why evaluation of improvement is below are above goal

BALANCE OF MATRIX DELETED

*Frequency of Evaluation
KEY: 1 = Annually; 2 = Every 2 years; 3 = Every 3 years; C = Continuous or Ongoing; S = Twice a year (fall & spring semester)

NOTE: "Evaluation Schedule for Reese Library," provides specific dates for evaluation of goals.
© *2000, Reese Library, Augusta State University*
• *For permission, contact Bill Nelson (wnelson@aug.edu) or Roxann Bustos (rbustos@aug.edu)*

Planning, Assessment, & Outcomes Assessment
(Evaluation)

Questions from the Standards, with some suggestions for a response.

1. Is the library's mission statement clearly understood by the library staff and the college administration? Is it reviewed periodically?
   - Develop a written statement:
     - ➢ Include immediate & long-range goals/objectives
     - ➢ Address the needs of Distance Learners
     - ➢ Outline the methods by which progress can be measured.

2. How does the library incorporate the college's mission into its goals and objectives?
   - Assess, using written profile of needs:
     - ➢ Availability and appropriateness of support
     - ➢ Library support for Distance Learners

3. Does the library maintain a systematic and continuous program:
     - ➢ for evaluating its performance,
     - ➢ for informing the college community of its accomplishments, and
     - ➢ for identifying and implementing needed improvements?

   - Regularly survey library users:
     - ➢ to monitor & assess both appropriateness of their use of services and resources, and
     - ➢ the degree to which the needs are being met.

4. Is the library's assessment plan an integral component of the institution's assessment and accreditation strategies?
   - Regularly survey library users:
     - ➢ to monitor & assess both appropriateness of their use of services and resources, and
     - ➢ the degree to which the needs are being met.

5. How does the library assess itself? (e.g. What quantitative and qualitative data does the library collect about its performance?)
   - Develop a written statement of goals and objectives
   - Outline the methods by which progress can be measured.

6. What outcomes does the library measure, and how does it measure these outcomes?
   - A primary outcome of distance learning is attainment of lifelong learning skills.
   - These skills can be assessed by information literacy competency standards.
   - Those standards are found at **http://www.ala.org/acrl/ilcomstan.html**

7. How does the library compare itself with its peers?
- Apply the ACRL Points of Comparison
- Example: Use material from **ratios** (Points of Comparison) for peer comparisons.
  - ➢ Identify peers
  - ➢ Retrieve peer data (using IPEDs, PALS, ACRL data, etc.)
  - ➢ Calculate ratios
  - ➢ Analyze results
  - ➢ Draw conclusions

Continuous Improvement:
Closing the Assessment Loop

- Review the Library mission statement.

- Review "Purposes" and "Goals."

- Review "Procedures for Evaluation" of each goal.

- Review "How Results are Used."

- Evaluate goals attainment.

- Use data generated to support budget requests for improvement of library services.

- Use the results from the assessment process as the basis for building a <u>revised</u> set of "Evaluation Procedures" and "Use of Results."

- The end result or goal is to demonstrate how the library contributes to teaching and learning at the institution.

- Repeat the process for continuous improvement.

Part II: Overview
Services, Instruction, Resources, Access, Staff, and Facilities

Introduction
This part of the workbook provides the core content for implementing the *Standards for College Libraries*, 2000 Edition, section-by-section beginning with Services. To properly view these six sections from an outcomes assessment perspective, and depict the relationship of outcomes and educational impact as these concepts pertain to the academic library, refer to the assessment diagram on page 42. This diagram outlines the framework for linking institutional goals to the library's role in two areas–assessing student learning and performing support functions–by defining and demonstrating the library's contributions to institutional effectiveness as outcomes or impacts. Immediately following this diagram is the Glossary of Key Assessment Topics and Terminology. Familiarize yourself with these terms, and then take the Strategic Planning Survey that follows the glossary.

Chapter Organization and Description
Each section begins with essential ideas for defining and measuring your library's contributions to institutional goals followed by a 3-column chart to depict the relationship among library principles, performance areas, and data sources. Key principles promulgated in the *Standards* (column 1) provide the framework for identifying corresponding and related performance areas (column 2) coupled to their data sources, tools and suggested points of comparison (column 3).

The next item in each section consists of checklists to facilitate responding to each section's evaluation questions from the *Standards*. The checklists provide information that a library may choose to use in answering specific questions. Included are suggested points of comparison, a new item in the *2000 Edition,* consisting of input and output measures used as ratios for peer comparison and longitudinal analysis. A library may selectively use these quantitative measures based on data collection methods, or modify according to the objectives or goals being supported. Which points of comparison a particular library chooses is strictly voluntary.

Next, use the above materials to aid in completing the worksheet for identifying measures of success applicable to your library. The purpose of the worksheet is to assist librarians and staff in identifying goals and objectives, and corresponding measures which could be used to evaluate success. Lastly, the following five sections-Services. Instruction, Resources, Access and Facilities- provide basic questions found in many user satisfaction surveys, and is based in part on work done at USC Aiken. For libraries interested in measuring service quality as a correlation of user satisfaction and user expectations, a description of LIBQUAL+ is provided on page 44.

What We Have Learned
Library assessment planning begins with a review of the institution strategic plan, vision, and mission statement which serve as the primary guiding documents. Linkage to specific

excerpts from the institution's mission, goals, and objectives should be clearly established in the library's mission statement, as well as its strategic plan and assessment plan. This is a key step in ensuring consistency between library activities, programs and initiatives and the purpose and goals of the institution. It provides the foundation for the library to identify how its own goals and objectives contribute to those of the institution, and how it is measuring the extent to which they are being achieved.

In some cases, this review will entail making recommendations to create assessment goals and objectives clearly linking the assessment of services and service quality to the library's attainment of its mission. Thus, the assessment process directly addresses the purpose of each library program and activity to include formulation of intended learning outcomes, development of assessment measures, data collection and analysis procedures, as well as using the results to make improvements.

Useful Tips for Getting Started
- Link library services, programs and activities (functions and processes) to institution goals and objectives
- Review each section's chart, essential ideas and checklists
- Complete the Worksheets for Identifying Measures of Success for Services, Instruction, Resources, Access, Staff and Facilities
- Select measures to be implemented for short and mid-range goals
- Select data collection method and develop/select tool to collect data
- For user surveys, review sample questions: Services, Instruction, Resources, Access, and Facilities, and ASU Graduating Student Survey
- Review Annotated Bibliography at Appendix A

Building a Continuous Improvement Model into Your Strategic Plan
The following statement and questions posed by Bede Mitchell, Dean of the Library and University Librarian, Zach S. Henderson Library, Georgia Southern University, provide a basic insight and rationale for assessment of outcomes and educational impact that can be attributed to college and university libraries as depicted on the next page:[1]

> The most effective and responsive service organizations strive constantly to improve. They implement systems to help them answer questions, such as:
> - What are we doing well?
> - What do we need to do better?
> - Should we be doing something else in order to achieve our vision?

Notes:
[1] Meeting with Bob Fernekes, on July 3rd, 2002.

Assessment of Outcomes and Educational Impact[1]

that can be attributed to College and University Libraries is grounded in

```
┌─────────────────────────────────────────────────────────────┐
│     Library Activities, Programs and Initiatives Designed To:│
└─────────────────────────────────────────────────────────────┘
```

```
┌──────────────────────────┐                ┌──────────────────────────────┐
│      Achieve Student      │      or        │       Contribute to          │
│     Learning Outcomes     │                │    Institutional Goals       │
│                           │                │      (in a support role)     │
└──────────────────────────┘                └──────────────────────────────┘
```

Course & Module Instruction[2]
Objectives Encompassing:

➢ Information Literacy[3]

➢ Information Technology[3]

➢ Course Research Requirements[4]

➢ Point-of-Need Assistance

➢ Graded Tutorials & Pathfinders
  with Quizzes

*See Section Charts[5] for Performance
Areas and Selected Measures:*

➢ Services
➢ Instruction
➢ Resources
➢ Access
➢ Staff
➢ Facility
➢ Communication & Cooperation
➢ Administration
➢ Budget

Notes:

[1] This diagram expands on a suggestion Bonnie Gratch-Lindauer makes in her article "Comparing the Regional Accreditation Standards: Outcomes Assessment and Other Trends," on page 20:

> Perhaps libraries should reserve the term "outcomes" for those measures and supporting documentation that provide evidence of student performance and proficiency related to information literacy skills, while using the term "impacts" or "effects" to document their other contributions to institutional goals.

[2] May be delivered in the classroom, online or one-to-one; includes assessing student learning.

[3] May be separate courses or integrated into core and discipline courses.

[4] Tailor instruction and assess outcomes linked to course assignments requiring the use of library and online resources.

[5] Use section charts in conjunction with evaluation questions and the worksheet for identifying measures of success. Collect data documenting educational impact from stakeholders, primarily through program reviews, surveys and focus groups, and use the points of comparison–inputs and outputs–for comparison with peers and longitudinal analysis.

Glossary of Key Assessment Topics and Terminology:
Focus on Library Assessment

Note: Refer to Appendix A for citations and short descriptions of sources mentioned below.

Assessment Plan: Different from an evaluation plan, the library assessment plan is a tool for measuring the effectiveness of the library in affecting learning outcomes. Tied to the educational mission of the institution and its campus-wide objectives, a learner-centered assessment plan for the library seeks to measure how and what library goals and objectives achieve in support of campus outcomes. See **Outcomes** and **Educational Impact**. Three noteworthy sources that develop these topics are Peter Hernon and Robert Dugan's *Action Plan for Outcomes Assessment in Your Library* published by ALA, and Bonnie Gratch-Lindauer's articles "Comparing the Regional Accreditation Standards: Outcomes Assessment and Other Trends" and "Defining and Measuring the Library's Impact on Campuswide Outcomes."

Balanced Scorecard: Developed by Robert S. Kaplan and David P. Norton, the balanced scorecard methodology is a management analysis technique designed to: (1) translate an organization's strategy and mission statement into–specific, measurable goals, activities undertaken to implement the strategy, and metrics to measure performance; (2) monitor the organization's performance in terms of achieving these goals across four perspectives: financial, customer, internal business processes, and learning and growth; (3) predict future performance; and (4) take proper actions to create the desired future. Those interested in applying the Balanced Scorecard in an academic library, should read Roswitha Poll's article "Performance, Processes and Costs: Managing Service Quality with the Balanced Scorecard."

Benchmarking: In the context of the *Standards for College Libraries*, 2000 Edition, the process of evaluating a library's points of comparison–inputs and outputs–against its peers and aspirational peers. Based on the goals of the variable being measured, the rank order of a library within its peer group may be used to indicate its success or need for improvement. See **Points of Comparison**.

Best Practices: Refers to those practices that have been shown to produce superior results or high performance, judged as successfully demonstrated, and can be adapted to fit another organization.

Educational Impact: Refers to measures which assess the library's contributions to institutional goals in a supporting role as distinct from performance indicators that assess student success, i.e., assess student learning resulting from librarian instruction or librarian prepared materials.

Evaluation of Assessment: This topic is concerned with evaluating the effectiveness of your assessment program, specifically the effectiveness of your assessment instruments. For example, if students can test out by taking an exam, compare the results of this group with those students that take a course to satisfy an information literacy requirement. Also, obtain faculty and student feedback in order to continually refine and improve your program and assessment tools.

Goal: Identifies what is to be accomplished. Using the assessment diagram on page 42, categorize your goals in each section as an outcome (assesses student learning), an educational impact (contributes to institutional goals in a support role) or other. Review any goals you may have placed in the other category.

Institutional Effectiveness: Used by institutions and regional accrediting agencies as an indicator of an institution's quality, i.e., a measure of its capability to accomplish its mission.

Institutional Quality Indicators: Two key indicators include the institution's ability and activities to assess its effectiveness, and then use this information to improve student learning, the scholarship of teaching and faculty development.

LIBQUAL+: As a research and development project, LIBQUAL+ key objectives include: (1) defining and measuring library service quality across institutions; (2) creating useful quality assessment tools for libraries; and (3) as an ARL New Measures Initiative pursue innovative ways for libraries to describe their contributions to their institutions. Statement adapted from LIBQUAL web page at **http://www.libqual.org/**

Measures of Success: Refers to the criteria your library has established for evaluating the extent to which a goal has been met. Create measures of success for your library Assessment Plan:
- To determine how well a program or service is achieving its goals.
- To define how performance will be measured along a scale or dimension.

Example Goals: Services & Instruction	Sample Measures of Success [illustration purposes]
Provide orientation to new faculty.	Positive feedback from faculty[1] [post-event survey]
Provide instruction (course/module/workshops) to target groups.	Learning objectives achieved[2] [end-of-semester assessment]; Example: 90% pass rate.

Notes:
[1] User Satisfaction Survey documents the effectiveness of orientation and impact.
[2] Assessment and analysis (by course, session, workshop, and number attending) documents learning objectives and outcomes attained as a result of librarian instruction.

Outcomes: As the first standards to introduce assessing outcomes, the *Standards for College Libraries*, 2000 Edition, uses the definition of outcomes provided in the 1998 ACRL *Task Force on Academic Library Outcomes Assessment Report*. This report views outcomes as . . ."*the ways in which library users are changed as a result of their contact with the library's resources and programs.*" Although recognizing satisfaction as an outcome, the report states:

The important outcomes of an academic library program involve answers to questions like these:
- Is the academic performance of students improved through their contact with the library?
- By using the library, do students improve their chances of having a successful career?
- Are undergraduates who used the library more likely to succeed in graduate school?
- Does the library's bibliographic instruction program result in a high level of "information literacy" among students?
- As a result of collaboration with the library's staff, are faculty members more likely to view use of the library as an integral part of their courses?
- Are students who use the library more likely to lead fuller and more satisfying lives?

Points of Comparison (Input and Output Measures): The *Standards for College Libraries*, 2000 Edition, replaces the use of input and output data as stand-alone indicators of performance (measured against arbitrary figures) with points of comparison (ratios of input and output data) for longitudinal analysis and peer comparison. The intent is for the library to select those points of comparison that it wishes to use in documenting its effectiveness over time (internal trend analysis), and its standing (rank order) measured against peers. Initially, it is envisioned that libraries will do a simple ratio analysis rather than perform a regression analysis.

Program Review: Refers to an institutions's periodic review of academic programs; provides a progress report on a program's achievement of strategic objectives. As an academic unit, the library's program review also provides an assessment in relation to strategic objectives.

Strategic Planning: Refers to the process that institutions perform, usually in concert with a program review, to identify priorities, themes, and objectives to be accomplished over a 5+ year period. It is critical for the library as an academic department to translate the institution's strategy, vision, and core values into specific goals and measures by establishing links to strategic plan themes and objectives. In turn, the program review coupled with other documentation provides a progress report on the institution's effectiveness. Strategic planning sets the tone for an institution as each level is completed. At Georgia Southern University, the strategic planning process consists of three levels: I, II & III. For example, Georgia Southern University Strategic Plan [Level I] is at **http://www2.gasou.edu/plan_ana/councils/guidance.htm** and Level II Planning is at **http://www2.gasou.edu/plan_ana/councils/SPLevIII.htm**. At other institutions, the highest level may be referred to as strategic, the middle level as operational, and the implementation level as tactical. For a practical solution on establishing links to your institution's strategic plan, complete the Strategic Planning Survey on the next page.

Strategic Planning Survey—Worksheet

1. In your own words, state your college or university's vision and core values:

_____

_____

_____

_____

_____

_____

_____

2. Next, identify institutional strategic themes or priorities which support your institution's vision and core values. Illustrative examples from Georgia Southern University's Strategic Plan include academic distinction, student-centered university, transcultural opportunities, technological advancement, public-private partnerships, and physical environment. Source: **http://www2.gasou.edu/plan_ana/councils/spc/stratplan.htm**

_____

_____

_____

_____

_____

_____

_____

_____

_____

_____

3. Is your library's strategic planning done as part of your institution's strategic planning and program review process? ☐ Yes   ☐ No

Standards and Assessment for Academic Libraries: A Workbook

Chapter 4
SERVICES

Contents:

> ➤ Essential ideas for defining and measuring your library's contribution to institutional goals
> ➤ Principles, performance areas and data sources
> ➤ Evaluation questions, including points of comparison
> ➤ Worksheet for identifying measures of success
> ➤ User survey sample questions including student information questions

Key Themes:

> ➤ Assessment planning begins with a review of the library mission statement in relation to the institution mission as part of the institution's strategic planning process

> ➤ Assessment of library services is a continuing process using variety of methods to evaluate the following:
> - *Educational impact contributing to the accomplishment of institutional goals*
> - *Range of services in support of the curriculum, student academic requirements, faculty development, research, and publication, and institution administrative requirements*
> - *Level of use and quality of services*
> - *Integration of library services with course instruction, and use of resources and learning spaces*
> - *Internet-based services licensed by the library for use by the academic community: interactive, push and on-demandtype services*

> ➤ Link the assessment of services to the library's attainment of its mission.

SERVICES

Essential Ideas for Defining and Measuring Your Library's Contributions to Institutional Goals

Review the performance chart (next page) in relation to your library services and programs, and begin mapping this information to your institutional goals and library mission statement. As explained in Part I, it is the responsibility of the library to define and describe how its goals, objectives and intended outcomes contribute to institutional goals. Accordingly, this section addresses the need for academic libraries to develop and use measures that assess and document the contribution/impact of library services and programs from an institutional perspective–student learning outcomes; faculty development, research and publication; and the teaching/learning environment.

Practical Solution: Develop assessment criteria and procedures for generating evidence of progress toward and/or achievement of library services and program goals as part of the library assessment plan.

Example Library Goals	Sample Measures of Success[1] [illustration purposes]
Provide orientation to new faculty	Positive feedback from faculty [post-event survey][2]
Demonstrate the educational impact of current awareness services	Positive feedback from faculty and students [post-event survey designed to measure impact][3]
Evaluate student products and processes to document information literacy skills	Increased use of reference assistance, and student portfolios consisting of better quality products [4]

Notes:

[1] Measures of success are defined as quality, effectiveness, performance and user satisfaction/ perception measures that can be used by academic librarians to develop a culture of evidence for documenting the library's contributions to institutional goals. Develop additional measures of success to support your library's goals using the section performance chart and worksheet.

[2] A User Satisfaction Survey documents the effectiveness of library orientation and impact. May be part of institution new faculty orientation. Working with new faculty provides an entry point for liaison activities, librarian instruction, and support of faculty research and publication.

[3] For this example consisting of multiple sessions and follow-up, there are three potential target groups: interested faculty (by department), undergraduate students enrolled in research courses, and graduate students enrolled in thesis courses. Growing in popularity, current awareness services provide users with requested tables of contents and citation alerts by e-mail as journals are published. Useful tool for identifying target journals to send a manuscript for publication, reviewing the literature, as well as covering journals not received.

[4] Make additional use of portfolios already being assembled by comparing achievement/growth of students receiving librarian assistance and/or instruction with those that do not. Moreover, some institutions may encourage the use of logs and submission of supporting information with research papers in order to evaluate student information seeking strategies as a process.

SERVICES

ACRL/CLS, *Standards* 2000 (Excerpt)	Performance Areas & Selected Measures	Data Sources & Applications
• The library should *establish, promote, maintain, and evaluate* a range of quality services that **support the college's mission and goals**	• **Quality and Effectiveness of:** ➤ **Range of Services**–ready reference, orientations/on demand tours, catalog/database searches, citation preparation, research assistance, consultations, online services (library and research guides, ask a librarian requests, virtual reference), assistance to call-in users, referrals, exhibits, special programs, troubleshooting assistance (network, email & online course login; printing, making copies, using microfilm/fiche machines), special services for different target groups.	• **Institution Mission and Goals:** focus on campus-wide goals and objectives for academic units and support services. For example, retention and graduate placement are receiving increased emphasis as accountability measures. • **Sources that identify user needs**, how well user needs are being met (surveys, comment forms, focus groups, self-study & accreditation reports), and methods of informing users of actions taken based on feedback (FAQs, web pages, student and faculty listservs, bulletins, and announcements in campus paper).
• The library should provide competent and prompt **assistance** for its users.	➤ **Service Desk Services** -Help Desks, Reference & Information Desks, Circulation, Reserves, Periodicals and Government Docs	
• **Reference and other special assistance** should be available at times when the college's primary users most need them. • **Hours of access to the library** should be reasonable and convenient for its users.	• Number of hours & time frames reference and other assistance is available. • Number of hours the library is open throughout the year; and during peak demand times, such as at the of a end of term.	• **User surveys and comparison with peers**: ➤ Library and Reference/Help Desk(s) hours of operation, types of services offered, and how these services are promoted and assessed. ➤ Suggested Points of Comparison-Output Measures
• When academic programs are offered at off-campus sites, **library services** should be provided in accordance with *ACRL Guidelines for Distance Learning Library Services.* **http://www.ala.org/acrl/guides/distlrng.html**	• **Quality and Effectiveness** of services in meeting information, bibliographic, and user needs - research assistance, consultations, access to online resources, materials on reserve, borrowing, interlibrary loan and document delivery services. • **Adequacy** of service hours.	➤ **Sources that identify distance learner needs**, how well these needs are being met (surveys, comment forms, focus groups, self-study & accreditation reports), and feedback to users.
See page 6 for complete citations.		

Services

Evaluation Questions (Extract from the Standards)
This section consists of eight questions from the Standards, and applicable checklists that you may want to consider as you review your library's services and assess quality of service. Use these checklists as a guide for identifying items to include in your response.

1. How well does the library establish, promote, maintain and evaluate a range of quality services that support the academic program of the college and optimal library use?

Range of library services: Hours of operation; User account services (obtain passwords, renew items checked out, and recall items); Reference services (assistance with finding, evaluating and using information in all formats, including print, Internet, online licensed databases, other special information resources; and orientation, ready reference, and referral services); Research services (on-demand, by appointment, in person, virtual, tele-phone, e-mail); Assistance with computer hardware, software, network, e-mail, and remote access services, Media and AV services; Disability services; Current awareness services; Access, borrowing, and reserve services, and Interlibrary loan, document delivery and related consortium services. For instruction services, see Instruction, Chapter 5.

2. Are reference, circulation, and government document services designed to enable users to take full advantage of the resources available to them?

Design of reference, circulation and government document services: Recognized as key service points, what makes these service areas stand out and facilitate their use, such as location, organization, signage, service hours, and capability to search specifically for reference resources, reserve resources, and government documents.

3. How do student and faculty expectations affect library services?

User expectations: Identify ways that are available for users to provide feedback, such as comment cards, Internet-based forms, focus groups, user surveys, and open door policy. Provide examples in which library services were changed or new services were added as a result of user feedback.

4. How well do interlibrary loan and document delivery services support the needs of qualified users?

Interlibrary loan and document delivery services: To determine how well these services support the needs of qualified users, use the following Output Measures (Suggested Points of Comparison) – Ratio of interlibrary loan requests to combined student and faculty FTE (could be divided between photocopies and books); Ratio of interlibrary loan lending to borrowing; Interlibrary loan/document delivery borrowing turnaround time, fill rate, and unit cost; Interlibrary loan/document delivery lending turnaround time, fill rate, and unit cost; and user feedback through surveys and comments.

5. Does the library maintain hours of access consistent with reasonable demand?

Hours of access: To determine if your library access hours are consistent with reasonable demand, compare your library hours with peers, and answer the following questions: (1) Is your library open a greater number of hours during peak demand, such as midterms and end of semester finals time, and (2) Are users satisfied with library hours?

6. What library services are provided for programs at off-campus sites? How are the needs of users and their satisfaction determined at those sites?

Library services for programs at off-campus sites: The *ACRL Guidelines for Distance Learning Library Services,* Fall 2000, list the following services: reference assistance; computer-based bibliographic and informational services; reliable, rapid, secure access to institutional and other networks including the Internet; consultation services; a program of library user instruction designed to instill independent and effective information literacy skills while specifically meeting the learner-support needs of the distance learning community; assistance with and instruction in the use of nonprint media and equipment; reciprocal or contractual borrowing, or interlibrary loan services using broadest application of fair use of copyrighted materials; prompt document delivery such as a courier system and/or electronic transmission; access to reserve materials in accordance with copyright fair use policies; adequate service hours for optimum access by users; and promotion of library services to the distance learning community, including documented and updated policies, regulations, and procedures for systematic development, and management of information resources.

User needs and satisfaction at off-campus sites: Identify ways that user needs are determined, and methods for users to provide feedback, such as comment cards, Internet-based forms, focus groups, user surveys, and open door policy.

7. How are students and faculty informed of library services?

Promotion and marketing of library services: Identify methods that your library uses to inform students and faculty of library services, such as student and faculty listservs; fliers and brochures distributed to clientele; short articles for campus news and college newspaper; program announcements; library orientations, library web site updates, and special columns and announcements; publicity through formal or informal liaison programs; displays and exhibits at the library; and a library services handbook.

8. Does the library maintain and utilize quantitative and qualitative measurements of its ability to serve its users?

Quantitative and qualitative measurements: Identify what measures you currently employ, such as use statistics (for example, the following Output Measure (Suggested Points of Comparison – Ratio of reference questions (sample week) to combined student and faculty FTE); interlibrary loan and document delivery data, and methods for users to provide feedback, such as comment cards, Internet-based forms, focus groups, and user surveys.

Worksheet for Identifying Measures of Success: Services

1. Examine your library goals and objectives. Select one that pertains to student academic success. Write this goal or objective in the space below.

_____

_____

_____

2. Does this goal or objective support your library mission statement?   ☐ Yes ☐ No

3. Check the *purpose(s)* that this goal or objective seeks to achieve (check all that apply):

☐ improve effectiveness   ☐ improve quality   ☐ improve user satisfaction
☐ assess outcomes   ☐ monitor progress   ☐ improve efficiency
☐ educational impact   ☐ retention   ☐ placement
☐ other (please explain): _____

4. Identify *measures* that would indicate that your library has successfully achieved the above goal or objective. Selected examples include: 75% coverage of a target group with orientations, consultations, special services; 10% increase compared to baseline or previous year data; favorable comparison with peer libraries (Evaluation Question #4), positive response to service quality and user satisfaction survey questions (set % goals for each question).

_____

_____

_____

_____

5. Review your response to question 4. Have you identified at least three measures of success that can be compared over time (longitudinally) for internal analysis and/or peer group comparison? Use this space to re-write your measures as applicable.

_____

_____

_____

_____

Standards and Assessment for Academic Libraries: A Workbook

6. Review data sources (for examples, see performance charts, column 3) to determine what is already being collected and by who, what needs to be collected, and suggested data collection methods. Use this space for comments or questions.

_____

_____

_____

_____

_____

_____

_____

_____

User Survey Sample Questions—Services

1. Student Status:
    - A. Freshman (less than 30 hours earned)
    - B. Sophomore (30-59 hours)
    - C. Junior (60-89 hours)
    - D. Senior (greater than 90 hours)
    - E. Other (e.g. non-degree or audit)

2. Age: A. 24 or below   B. 25 or above

3. Purpose of Most Recent Library Visit:
    - A. Academic/course research or reading
    - B. Personal interest research or reading
    - C. Quiet study
    - D. Group study/class visit
    - E. Other _____

User Survey Sample Questions—Services
Please indicate your level of satisfaction by selecting one of the following choices [strongly agree **(SA)**, agree **(A)**, neutral **(N)**, disagree **(D)**, strongly disagree **(SD)**, and not applicable **(NA)**] to describe whether you received attentive, courteous, and helpful assistance from the following service areas:

	SA	A	N	D	SD	NA
1. Circulation & Reserves personnel						
2. Reference personnel						
3. Periodicals personnel						
4. U.S. and State Documents personnel						
5. Interlibrary Loan personnel						

6. Have you used the Interlibrary Loan service to obtain materials from other libraries?
A. Frequently   B. Infrequently   C. Never
If you answered A or B to question 6, also answer questions 7 & 8 as applicable, otherwise skip to question 9.

7. If you have used Interlibrary Loan to request a book, were you satisfied with the results?
A. Yes   B. No

8. If you have used Interlibrary Loan to request a journal article, were you satisfied with the results?   A. Yes   B. No

9. If you have never used Interlibrary Loan, indicate your reason:
    - A. I obtain what I need from our library or online
    - B. I obtain what I need by going to other libraries
    - C. I did not know about Interlibrary Loan service
    - D. Other reasons (Please explain in the write-in area on your answer sheet)

Chapter 5
INSTRUCTION

Contents:

> ➢ Essential ideas for defining and measuring your library's contribution to institutional goals
> ➢ Principles, performance areas and data sources
> ➢ Evaluation questions, including points of comparison
> ➢ Instruction survey
> ➢ Instruction assessment activity checklist
> ➢ Worksheet for identifying measures of success
> ➢ User survey sample questions

Key Themes:

> ➢ Assessment planning begins with a review of the library mission statement in relation to the institution mission as part of the institution's strategic planning process

> ➢ Assessment of librarian instruction is a continuing process using a variety of methods to evaluate the following:
> - *Achievement of learning outcomes*
> - *Educational impact of instructional services*
> - *Range of instructional services in support of the curriculum, student academic requirements, faculty development, research, and publication, and institution administrative requirements*
> - *Reach and quality of librarian instruction*
> - *Integration of library and information skills instruction into the curriculum coupled with the use of resources and learning spaces*

> ➢ Link the assessment of instruction, i.e., the assessment of learning outcomes and educational impact, to the library's attainment of its mission.

INSTRUCTION

Essential Ideas for Defining and Measuring Your Library's Contributions to Institutional Goals

Review the performance chart (next page) in relation to your library's instruction offerings, and begin mapping this information to your institutional goals and library mission statement. As explained in Part I, it is the responsibility of the library to define and describe how its goals, objectives and intended outcomes contribute to institutional goals. Accordingly, this section addresses the need for academic libraries to develop and use measures that assess and document the contribution/impact of librarian instruction from an institutional perspective–student learning outcomes; faculty development, research and publication; and the teaching/learning environment.

Practical Solution: Develop assessment criteria and procedures for generating evidence of progress toward and/or achievement of library instruction/program goals as part of the library assessment plan.

Example Library Goals	Sample Measures of Success[1] [illustration purposes]
Design and produce instruction materials	Research outcomes achieved using research guides/pathfinders[2] [observation/end-of-semester review]
Provide instruction (course/module/workshops) to target groups	Learning objectives achieved[3] [end-of-semester and module assessments]; Example: 90% pass rate
Instruct information literacy course/modules	Learning outcomes achieved[4] [Pre- and post-tests of basic and advanced skills]

Notes:

[1] Measures of success are defined as quality, effectiveness, performance and user satisfaction/ perception measures that can be used by academic librarians to develop a culture of evidence documenting the library's contributions to institutional goals. Develop additional measures of success to support your library's goals using section materials.

[2] In this example, instruction materials include research guides and pathfinders tailored to specific course research requirements. Students are observed using handouts/printouts or online instruction materials to access library and online resources. The end-of-semester review consists of the course instructor's evaluation of completed research papers using the following criteria: appropriate resources cited and data/information used from these sources appears to be complete and accurate. Using these criteria, the measure of success could be an improvement in student grades of 5% or 10% on the research assignment compared against baseline data.

[3] Assessment and analysis (by course, session, workshop, and number attending) documents learning objectives and outcomes attained as a result of librarian instruction. This example encompasses bibliographic, information literacy and information technology instruction, and may support institution retention objectives depending on target groups selected.

[4] By design, assessment methods measure information literacy competencies. Visit the ACRL Information Literacy website at http://www.csusm.edu/acrl/il/index.html

INSTRUCTION

ACRL/CLS, *Standards* 2000 (Excerpt)	Performance Areas & Selected Measures	Data Sources & Applications
• As an **academic unit** within the college, the library should <u>facilitate academic success</u>, as well as <u>encourage lifelong learning</u>. • **Librarians** should <u>collaborate frequently with classroom faculty</u>; they should <u>participate in curriculum planning</u>, as well as <u>educational outcomes assessment</u>.	• **Student Academic Success:** ➢ Quality and Effectiveness of: — Research assistance — Instruction — Research guides & pathfinders ➢ Assessment of course work requiring research/IT skills: — Learning objectives and outcomes to be attained as a result of librarian instruction — Pathfinders keyed to specific course research requirements	• **Collaboration** ➢ Faculty liaison activities ➢ Point-of-need & end-of-course student and faculty surveys ➢ Usability surveys ➢ Portfolios- course assignments, bibliographies, papers, self-paced learning tutorials, workbooks or web modules, and projects that underscore research process. ➢ **User surveys**
• **Modes of instruction** . . . may include, but are not limited . . .	➢ Mode of instruction tailored to information need	➢ **User surveys**
• The library should provide **information** and **instruction** to users through a <u>variety of reference and bibliographic services</u>, such as course-related and integrated instruction, hands-on active learning, orientations, formal courses, tutorials, pathfinders, and point-of-use instruction, including the reference interview.	• **Integration of Services and Resources into Curriculum:** ➢ Attendance at orientations, bibliographic instruction sessions & workshops designed to support curriculum requirements: — number of users attending — percentage of target group ➢ Development of IT skills oriented hands-on instruction ➢ Number of courses (%) by department requiring research.	• **Instruction Assessment Activitites Checklist** ➢ Attendance rosters, instruction schedules, academic department and registrar records to identify target groups, such as freshmen, transfer students, specific majors, students enrolled in selected courses/programs, graduating seniors, and distance learners ➢ Course syllabi and assignments for research components
• **Information literacy skills** and **bibliographic instruction** should be <u>integrated</u> into appropriate courses with special attention given to intellectual property, copyright, and plagiarism.	• **Instruction and Application of Information Literacy Skills:** ➢ Number of courses (%) by department- integrated instruction ➢ Information literacy course(s)	• **Instruction Assessment Activitites Checklist** ➢ Course syllabi and assignments ➢ User self-assessments, and competency pre- and post-tests.
	• **Faculty Development:** ➢ Research Collaboration ➢ Current Awareness Services ➢ Special workshops	• **Faculty liaison activities** ➢ Articles & books published ➢ Faculty surveys
See page 6 for complete citations.		

Instruction

Evaluation Questions (Extract from the Standards)
This section consists of seven questions from the Standards, and applicable checklists that you may want to consider as you review your library's services and assess quality of service. Use these checklists as a guide for identifying items to include in your response.

1. Does the library provide formal and informal opportunities for instruction?

Formal Instruction includes guided tours, orientations, course-related instruction, course-integrated instruction, information literacy tutorials, information literacy course, research skills tutorials, library skills (research) courses, seminars and workshops. For each type of instruction, identify its title, frequency, attendance, and whether it includes hands-on active learning. *Suggested Points of Comparison: Input measures –*
Ratio of number of students attending library instructional sessions to total number of students in target group.

Informal Instruction includes reference desk interviews, help desk assistance, point-of-use assistance, virtual reference, self-guided tours, and instruction provided by telephone, e-mail, and pathfinders.

2. Does the library provide adequate space for instruction for both large and small groups? Is the available space designed to provide hands-on instruction, as well as presentation of all types of resources?

Space for Instruction: Identify areas used for formal instruction, such as lecture rooms, auditorium, electronic classrooms, and computer labs. Review accreditation reports, library strategic plan, library annual report, and institution program review documents for information on instructional space requirements, shortfalls, and projected needs.

3. Does the library make appropriate use of technology in its instruction?

Technology available to instructors:

---

4. How do librarians work with classroom faculty in developing and evaluating library curricula in support of specific courses?

Applicable Liaison Activities include reviewing course syllabi and course assignments and collaborating with classroom faculty in order to accomplish the following: evaluate library resources and licensed databases in relation to specific research requirements and learning outcomes, update and tailor subject guides and pathfinders to course needs, schedule workshops on relevant resources, create a course assignment that develops research skills, teach a class on research methods and resources that responds to a specific course assignment or information needs.

Library Orientation of New Students. This area includes participation in courses designed to orient new students to academia and the resources available to them as students.

Information Literacy. Describe your library's efforts in facilitating and instructing information literacy skills.

5. If applicable, how does the library facilitate faculty research?

If yes, *identify activities* in this area. Consider the potential of current awareness services, such as ingenta.com, in keeping your faculty abreast of current research in their respective areas, and for identifying journals where they might consider submitting articles for publication.

6. Does the library provide a variety of educational programs?

If yes, *identify your educational programs* to include workshops and seminars.

7. How does the library promote and evaluate its instructional programs?

Promotion and marketing of instructional programs: Identify methods that your library uses to inform students and faculty of library services, such as student and faculty listservs; fliers and brochures distributed to clientele; short articles for campus news and college newspaper; program announcements; library orientations, library web site updates, and special columns and announcements; publicity through formal or informal liaison programs; displays and exhibits at the library; and a library services handbook.

Evaluation of instructional programs: Identify methods that your library uses to evaluate its instructional programs, such as evaluation by users, classroom faculty, colleagues and other librarians. Attach copies of evaluation forms. An example form for obtaining immediate participant feedback is found on the next page.

*The Instruction Survey (next page) was developed by Sonya Gaither Shepherd and Bob Fernekes, and approved for implementation by Information Services librarians at Georgia Southern University in the Spring Semester 2002.

Participant Status: ☐ Student ☐ Faculty ☐ Staff ☐ Other

Instruction Survey – _____

Title of Instruction and Name of Librarian

Please evaluate each item (indicate your level of satisfaction) by selecting one of the following choices [strongly agree (**SA**), agree (**A**), neutral (**N**), disagree (**D**), strongly disagree (**SD**), and Not Applicable (**NA**)]:

	SA	A	N	D	SD	NA
The purpose of the instruction was clearly defined.						
The key points of instruction were achieved.						
The instruction was relevant and useful.						
The instruction was clear and understandable.						
The handouts were relevant and useful.						
Online pathfinders (guides) were relevant and useful.						
I gained new and useful information for my assignment.						
The length of instruction was appropriate for the content covered.						
The format (demonstration or hands-on) used was appropriate for the content covered.						
I plan to use my newly acquired knowledge and skills during the next month.						

I would recommend this instruction: ☐ Yes ☐ No Explain: _____

The instruction provided allowed for hands-on practice? ☐ Yes ☐ No
I would like additional assistance or advanced instruction on the following: _____

_____

How could this presentation be improved? _____

_____

Other comments:_____

_____

If software instruction, was your attendance at this workshop voluntary? ☐ Yes ☐ No

If software instruction, how often do you use this software?
☐ Never ☐ Daily ☐ Weekly ☐ Monthly

Instruction Assessment Activity Checklist

Integration of Library and Online Resources into the Curriculum

_____ # of courses in which course syllabus/handouts identify research requirements.

_____ # of courses in which course syllabus/handouts identify resources.

_____ # of courses supported by a librarian developed research guide/course pathfinder that links resources (and how to help) to specific research requirements.

_____ # of courses in which course syllabus/handouts provide links to above research guides or course pathfinders.

_____ # of courses supported by librarian instruction session.

Note: As program expands, create a spreadsheet showing department, course title, section and instructor. Maintain copies or links to course syllabus, and instructor/librarian prepared handouts.

User Reaction to Librarian Instruction and One-To-One Assistance

☐ Satisfaction Survey ☐ Focus Groups ☐ Term Paper Assessment
☐ Service Quality Survey ☐ Portfolio Assessment ☐ End-of-Course Assessment
☐ Course Research Learning Outcomes Assessment

Other methods:

_____

_____

_____

Assessment of Information Literacy & Information Technology Learning Outcomes

☐ Pre-Test ☐ Self-Assessment ☐ Portfolio Requirements
☐ Post-Test ☐ Graded Exercises ☐ Separate Course
☐ Workshops ☐ Certification Exam ☐ Freshman Year Experience

Other methods/success stories:

_____

_____

_____

_____

_____

_____

_____

Worksheet for Identifying Measures of Success: Instruction

1. Examine your library goals and objectives. Select one that pertains to student academic success. Write this goal or objective in the space below.

_____

_____

_____

2. Does this goal or objective support your library mission statement? ☐ Yes ☐ No

3. Check the *purpose(s)* that this goal or objective seeks to achieve (check all that apply):

☐ improve effectiveness   ☐ improve quality   ☐ improve user satisfaction
☐ assess outcomes   ☐ monitor progress   ☐ improve efficiency
☐ educational impact   ☐ retention   ☐ placement
☐ other (please explain): _____

4. Identify *measures* that would indicate that your library has successfully achieved the above goal or objective. Selected examples include: 100% coverage of a target group, such as new faculty during orientations; number of courses (%) by department with research requirements/integrated information literacy instruction; 90% information literacy course pass rate; identification/achievement of learning objectives and outcomes attained (by course, workshop, and number attending) as a result of librarian instruction; and 5% increase in attendance compared to baseline.

_____

_____

_____

_____

5. Review your response to question 4. Have you identified at least three measures of success that can be compared over time (longitudinally) for internal analysis and/or peer group comparison? Use this space to re-write your measures as applicable.

_____

_____

_____

_____

_____

Standards and Assessment for Academic Libraries: A Workbook

6. Review data sources (for examples, see performance chart, column 3) to determine what is already being collected and by who, what needs to be collected, and suggested data collection methods. Use this space for comments or questions.

_____

_____

_____

_____

_____

_____

_____

_____

_____

User Survey Sample Questions—Instruction

1. Has a librarian given a library user orientation or demonstration of library resources (print or online/CD-ROM databases) to any of your courses? ☐ Yes ☐ No

If you answered No to question 1, please skip to next section. If you answered Yes to question 1, please select one of the following choices [strongly agree **(SA)**, agree **(A)**, neutral **(N)**, disagree **(D)**, strongly disagree **(SD)**, and not applicable **(NA)**] to evaluate (self-assess) whether the library/research instruction gave you an adequate understanding or skill in using the following:

	SA	A	N	D	SD	NA
the library catalog for locating resources in the library, as well as resources in system libraries.						
licensed databases for locating citations and abstracts, and full text journal, magazine, newspaper, and reference sources						
general and specialized print sources located in the library reference area (e.g. almanacs, biographies, directories, encyclopedic-type sources) for locating subject/discipline information, citations, abstracts, and bibliographies.						
the Internet for locating resources pertinent to course requirements.						

Chapter 6
RESOURCES

Contents:

> ➤ Essential ideas for defining and measuring your library's contribution to institutional goals
> ➤ Principles, performance areas and data sources
> ➤ Evaluation questions, including points of comparison
> ➤ Worksheet for identifying measures of success
> ➤ User survey sample questions

Key Themes:

> ➤ Assessment planning begins with a review of the library mission statement in relation to the institution mission as part of the institution's strategic planning process

> ➤ Assessment of library owned and licensed resources is a continuing process using a variety of methods to evaluate the following:
> * *Educational impact contributing to the accomplishment of institutional goals*
> * *Scope and depth of resources (strengths and weaknesses) in support of each discipline/major, student academic requirements, faculty development, research, and publication, and institution administrative requirements*
> * *Level of use and quality of resources*
> * *Integration of resources into course instruction and learning spaces*
> * *Migration to online resources and networked CDs*

> ➤ Link the assessment of library owned and licensed resources to the library's attainment of its mission.

RESOURCES

Essential Ideas for Defining and Measuring Your Library's Contributions to Institutional Goals

Review the performance chart (next page) in relation to your library's collection development plan and begin mapping this information to your institutional goals and library mission statement. As explained in Part I, it is the responsibility of the library to define and describe how its goals, objectives and intended outcomes contribute to institutional goals. Accordingly, this section addresses the need for academic libraries to develop and use measures that assess and document the contribution/impact of the library's collection and online licensed resources from an institutional perspective–student learning outcomes; faculty development, research and publication; and the teaching/learning environment.

Practical Solution: As part of the library assessment plan, develop assessment criteria and procedures for generating evidence of progress toward and/or achievement of the library's goals covering collection development to include acquiring access to online resources.

Example Library Goals	Sample Measures of Success[1] [illustration purposes]
Provide library and electronic resources integral to the current and future success of the institution	Use two assessment approaches: collection-centered and user/use-based. Compare your results with metrics and measures you have established for each approach[2]
Ensure sufficient library support for new courses and programs	Library and electronic resources identified and provided [according to collection development plan/faculty collaboration][3]
Participate in cooperative collection development efforts to increase scope and depth of information resources supporting the curriculum and research	Active member of key consortia–degree of success in: selecting/funding shared purchases/licensing resources, supporting assigned research-level subject areas, and retaining core journal titles and reference resources per a "protected titles" policy[4]

Notes:

[1] Measures of success are defined as quality, effectiveness, performance and user satisfaction/ perception measures that can be used by academic librarians to develop a culture of evidence documenting the library's contributions to institutional goals. Use the section worksheet to develop and refine measures of success to support your library's goals.

[2] Use a conspectus-like methodology of divisions, categories, subjects, and rating codes (0-5, to indicate out of scope, minimal, basic information, study or instructional support, research and comprehensive levels, respectively) to compare the strength of your current collection against the intended outcomes of your collection development goals, as well as acquisition and preservation commitments. Then, compare this assessment with user survey results and usage data measures of success coupled with descriptive comments on subject strengths or limits.

[3] Identify key resources using title lists and comparison with peer library resources.

[4] Document the benefits/advantages of local area and statewide library and institution consortia.

RESOURCES

ACRL/CLS, *Standards* 2000 (Excerpt)	Performance Areas & Selected Measures	Data Sources & Applications
• **Nature & Purpose**–The library should provide varied, authoritative and up-to-date resources that support its mission and the needs of its users.	• **Library resources and licensed databases integral to the current and future success of the college.** ➢ **Criteria** used to make decisions about the selection, acquisition, retention, and use of resources -approval plans, profiles, standing orders, title lists, reviews, course syllabus, comparison with other libraries, collection level codes, consortia agreements, and faculty recommendations. ➢ Consortium ordering & licensing	• **Institution documents and external reports,** such as institution strategic plan, self study, and program reviews, and accreditation reports by regional and professional organizations: ➢ Strengths and weaknesses ➢ Strategic priorities ➢ **Library policies** and criteria on selection, acquisition, retention and use of resources. ➢ **Agreements** (scope & savings)
• **Currency**–Collection currency and vitality should be maintained through judicious weeding.	• **Effective Evaluation Program:** ➢ Collection-based techniques –comparison with lists and other libraries, collection level codes,direct examination, Suggested Points of Comparisons – Input Measures. ➢ Use-based measures – in-library use, and Suggested Points of Comparison – Output Measures	• **Measures** on left to evaluate collection by discipline, subject and course as appropriate. • **ACRL & IPEDS data** (when possible) for longitudinal and comparison with peers: Suggested Points of Comparison- Input & Output Measures, Evaluation, Question #8.
• **Format Selection** –Resources may be in a variety of formats, including print or hard copy, online electronic texts or images, and other media. Within budget constraints, the library should provide quality resources in the most efficient manner possible. • **Physical Locations** –Resources may be provided onsite or from remote storage locations, on the main campus or at off-campus locations.	• **Optimal blend of resources —print, electronic and media:** ➢ Sufficiency of collections and licensed databases –subject, level of content & currency to support: — Curriculum requirements: student research/practitioner competencies, productivity, and tools for analysis and evaluation — Faculty research needs — Balanced reference collection — Recreational reading and news ➢ Sufficient # of user licenses for on campus and remote access	• **User surveys & focus groups** ➢ Curriculum documents covering program and course resource requirements, reading lists ➢ Employer & alumni surveys ➢ Faculty publications & liaison ➢ Peer comparison ➢ Lifelong learning documents ➢ Online database usage data

See page 6 for complete citations.

Resources

Evaluation Questions (Extract from the Standards)
This section consists of nine questions from the Standards, and applicable checklists that you may want to consider as you review your library collection development assessment policy and procedures. Use these checklists as a guide for identifying items to include in your response.

1. What criteria are used to make decisions about the acquisition, retention, and use of print, electronic, and media resources? How does the library select resources for its users?

Selection criteria for book resources (Print and Ebooks): Approval & Selection Plans, Profiles, Priorities & Standing Orders, Book Lists, Book Reviews, Classroom Faculty Recommendations, Classroom Faculty Research, Collection Level Codes, Comparison with other Library Collections, Consortia Agreements, Course Syllabus Reading and Research Requirements, Distance Learning Support, and Student Recommendations.

Selection Criteria for Periodicals, including Newspapers (Print, Full-Text/Full-Image & Electronic Resources: Classroom Faculty Recommendations, Comparison with other Library Collections, Consortia Agreements, Course Syllabus/Research, Distance Learning Support, and Periodical Lists.

Selection Criteria for Other Print Resources: Institution Archives, Government Publications Depository (State, United States, Other), and Graduate Thesis.

Selection Criteria for Multimedia (Videos, Films, Maps, etc.): Classroom Faculty Recommendations, Comparison with other Library Collections, Course Syllabus, Distance Learning Support, and Reviews.
Organization & Use From a User Perspective: Browsing Area, Circulating Book Collection, Curriculum Lab, Distance Learning Collection(s), Electronic Resources, Government Documents, Multimedia, Online Resources, Periodicals (Current, Bound & Microfilm), Reference Collection, Reserves, and Special Collection(s).

Retention or Deselection Policy/Procedure: Browsing Area, Circulating Book Collection, Curriculum Lab, Distance Learning Collection(s), Electronic Resources, Government Documents, Multimedia, Online Resources, Periodicals (Current, Bound & Microfilm), Reference Collection, Reserves, and Special Collections(s).

2. What is the role of the classroom faculty in the selection of library resources and in the ongoing development and evaluation of the collection?

Role of Academic Department Library Representatives and Classroom Faculty:
specific responsibilities identified in library policies/procedures.

Roles when the following occur: budget shortfall, changes in consortia agreements, institution undergoes a program review, new courses added, new programs added, and other roles.

Service Quality and Satisfaction (User Survey – Faculty): library support of course needs and faculty research needs.

3. Does the library have a continuing and effective program to evaluate its collections, resources and online databases, both quantitatively and qualitatively?

Evaluation Using Collection-Based Techniques: comparison of library collection with lists (identify lists), comparison by title with other library collections, comparison by title with other library online databases, conspectus evaluation–use of collection level codes, direct examination of the collection, suggested points of comparison using input measures, and support of distance education.

Evaluation – Use-Based Measures: in-library use (reference resources, periodicals, reserves, etc.), and suggested points of comparison using output measures.

Service Quality and Satisfaction (User Survey – Students): sufficiency of collections and licensed databases.

Service Quality and Satisfaction (User Survey – Faculty): library support of course needs and faculty research needs.

Service Quality and Satisfaction (User Survey – Staff): library support of institution research needs.

4. Do print, media, and electronic resources reflect campus curricular and research needs?

Curriculum Needs: Institution Program Reviews, Institution Self Study, Library Annual Report, Regional Accreditation Report/Visit, Professional Accreditation Report/Visit, and Classroom Faculty input. Use these sources to provide information on specific programs to be enhanced with library resources, to identify significant resources that have been added to the collection or licensed, and to identify how specific shortfalls in library and online resources are being addressed.

Faculty Research Needs: library, licensed and consortia resources, current awareness services, document delivery, and interlibrary loan. Identify your method for checking how well faculty research needs are being met through a combination of library resources and services.

5. Does the library have sufficient user licenses for its electronic resources so that on-site and remote users can be accommodated?

Licenses for Electronic Resources: Identify databases limited to library and on-site use, identify number of concurrent users by database, identify proxy server concurrent user capability, identify procedure for increasing number of users for hands-on training, and identify remote user access requirements, such as plug-in, user ID, and password.

6. How are consortium purchasing and licensing agreements utilized?

Consortium Agreements: Identify your library consortium agreements, and how these agreements support curricular and faculty research needs.

7. If the library has responsibility for collecting and maintaining the college archives, how does it address these responsibilities?

Identify applicable policies and guidelines.

8. How do the library's collections and online databases compare with its peers?

Collection comparisons: Use the following methods–
Suggested Points of comparison: Input measures:
- Ratio of volumes to combined total student (undergraduate & graduate) & faculty FTE;
- Ratio of volumes added per year to combined total student and faculty FTE;
- Ratio of material/information resource expenditures to combined total student and faculty FTE; and
- Percent of total library budget expended for materials/information resources, subdivided by print, microform, and electronic.

Suggested Points of comparison: Output measures:
- Ratio of circulation (excluding reserves) to combined student and faculty FTE.
- Ratio of interlibrary loan requests to combined student and faculty FTE (could be divided between photocopies and books).
- Ratio of interlibrary loan lending to borrowing.

Collection Title Lists: For selected areas or disciplines requiring special emphasis.

Online databases comparisons: For selected areas or disciplines requiring special emphasis, identify consortium and institution licensed databases.

9. Does the library maintain the currency of the collection through a judicious weeding program?

Provide documentation to support response.

Worksheet for Identifying Measures of Success: Resources

1. Examine your library goals and objectives. Select one that pertains to providing resources that support the college mission and needs of users. Write this goal or objective in the space below.

_____

_____

_____

2. Does this goal or objective support your library mission statement?   ☐ Yes ☐ No

3. Check the *purpose(s)* that this goal or objective seeks to achieve (check all that apply):

☐ improve effectiveness   ☐ improve quality   ☐ improve user satisfaction
☐ assess outcomes   ☐ monitor progress   ☐ improve efficiency
☐ educational impact   ☐ retention   ☐ placement
☐ other (please explain): _____

4. Identify *measures* that would indicate that your library has successfully achieved the above goal or objective. Selected examples include: balanced reference collection/ circulating collection/licensed databases (meet course syllabus requirements, and key titles compared to title lists/peer library holdings); favorable comparison with peer libraries using suggested points of comparison (Evaluation Question #8); positive response to service quality and user satisfaction survey questions (set % goals for each question); and maintain or increase funding compared to previous year data.

_____

_____

_____

_____

5. Review your response to question 4. Have you identified at least three measures of success that can be compared over time (longitudinally) for internal analysis and/or peer group comparison? Use this space to re-write your measures as applicable.

_____

_____

_____

_____

_____

6. Review data sources (for examples, see performance chart, column 3) to determine what is already being collected and by who, what needs to be collected, and suggested data collection methods. Use this space for comments or questions.

_____

_____

_____

_____

_____

_____

_____

_____

_____

User Survey Sample Questions—Resources

Please indicate your level of satisfaction by selecting one of the following choices [strongly agree **(SA)**, agree **(A)**, neutral **(N)**, disagree **(D)**, strongly disagree **(SD)**, and not applicable **(NA)**] to describe whether the following items are generally satisfactory for meeting your course needs:

	SA	A	N	D	SD	NA
Circulating book collection						
Reference book collection						
Journals and magazines (current issues and back files) and full text online						
Newspapers and full text online						
Federal and State Documents collections and online government resources						

For an example online satisfaction survey tailored to resources and accessibility, try the Zach S. Henderson Library satisfaction survey at http://www2.gasou.edu/library/surveys/satisfaction_survey.html

Chapter 7
ACCESS

Contents:

- ➢ Essential ideas for defining and measuring your library's contribution to institutional goals
- ➢ Principles, performance areas and data sources
- ➢ Evaluation questions, including points of comparison
- ➢ Worksheet for identifying measures of success
- ➢ User survey sample questions

Key Themes:

- ➢ Assessment planning begins with a review of the library mission statement in relation to the institution mission as part of the institution's strategic planning process

- ➢ Assessment of access to library owned and licensed resources is a continuing process using a variety of methods to evaluate the achievement of library and institution goals pertaining to the following:
  - *Ease of use and accuracy of the library catalog and ease of navigation between the catalog, online databases, online library information, and library catalogs of other institutions with borrowing agreements*
  - *Support of distant learners*
  - *Improved physical accessibility as a means to organize resources to support learning communities*
  - *Access to online full-text/image sources*
  - *Access to data for statistical analysis*

- ➢ Link the assessment of access to library owned and licensed resources to the library's attainment of its mission.

ACCESS

Essential Ideas for Defining and Measuring Your Library's Contributions to Institutional Goals

Review the performance chart (next page) in relation to your library's access goals, and begin mapping this information to your institutional goals and library mission statement. As explained in Part I, it is the responsibility of the library to define and describe how its goals, objectives and intended outcomes contribute to institutional goals. Accordingly, this section addresses the need for academic libraries to develop and use measures that assess and document the contribution/ impact of the library's access function/process from an institutional perspective–student learning outcomes; faculty development, research and publication; and the teaching/learning environment. Access encompasses both intellectual and physical accessibility. It includes familiar services such as circulation, reserves, direct borrowing from other libraries, interlibrary loan, document delivery, and distant learner, remote access, portal and current awareness services. It also includes methods and applications to improve accessibility such as new and enhanced library catalog and database features to locate, obtain and manage information and user accounts.

Practical Solution: Develop assessment criteria and procedures for generating evidence of progress toward and/or achievement of the library's access goals as part of the library assessment plan.

Example Library Goals	**Sample Measures of Success**[1] [illustration purposes]
Improve online access to and use of library resources and information–facility, campus and remote access	Enhanced web access to library catalog, databases, and to other online research tools through vendor integrated system; Expanded electronic reserves
Organize/maintain library services, resources and equipment for efficient access by library users	Improved physical access to services, resources and information–signage, layout of book stacks and study/computer areas, shelving accuracy, etc.
Develop/maintain a holistic, seamless computing environment integrating access, media, and software applications	New goal. Improved service quality/user satisfaction compared with baseline assessment[2]

Notes:
[1] Measures of success are defined as quality, effectiveness, performance and user satisfaction/ perception measures that can be used by academic librarians to develop a culture of evidence documenting the library's contributions to institutional goals. Using section materials, develop additional measures of success to support your library's goals.
[2] This example of a campus library as a research and study/computing facility covers the spectrum of computing capabilities needed to support an evolving curriculum. Conduct a needs analysis to determine technology requirements, compare with peer libraries, develop a library technology plan, seek funding, and implement as an integral element of the library and institution strategic plans.

ACCESS

ACRL/CLS, *Standards* 2000 (Excerpt)	Performance Areas & Selected Measures	Data Sources & Applications
• **Access to library resources** should be provided in a <u>timely</u> and <u>orderly</u> fashion. • A **central catalog of library resources** should provide access for multiple concurrent users and clearly indicate <u>all resources</u>	• **Service Quality & Satisfaction:** ➤ **Ease of accessing** library catalog & online licensed resources from the library, campus & remote locations. ➤ Ability to locate desired information ➤ Accuracy, currency, integration of library catalog, licensed databases and online sources.	• **User surveys & focus groups** • **Library program review** • **Catalog study** • **Library strategic plan**: provide seamless access
• **Provision** should be made for <u>interlibrary loan</u>, <u>consortial borrowing agreements</u>, access to <u>virtual electronic collections</u>, and <u>document delivery</u> to provide access to materials not owned . . .	• **Services** relating to access: look up call number, locate item in library, assistance in using library catalog and licensed databases, telephone support, and use of library reserves, electronic reserves, Interlibrary loan, document delivery, and consortium borrowing.	• **User surveys & focus groups** • **Comparison with peers**: — Services offered & how services are assessed. Suggested Points of Comparison - Output Measures, Evaluation Question #4.
• Furthermore, **distance learning programs** should be supported by equivalent means such as <u>remote electronic access</u> to collections, the provision of <u>reliable network connections</u>, and <u>electronic transmission</u> or <u>courier delivery</u> of library materials to remote users.	• Library **web page organization** and **instructions** for: ➤ accessing databases, full text/image resources & electronic journals from library, campus & remote locations ➤ finding and using research guides ➤ accessing remote user and distance learner information and services	• **User surveys & focus groups** • **Web usability studies** • **Remote access** documentation: proxy server authentication requirements (IP recognition, plug-in, user ID & password)
• **Policies** regarding access should be appropriately disseminated to library users.	• Measures relating to **computers**: ➤ Number of computers in library and on campus for student use. ➤ Standard computer configuration to include software applications and CD availability on library computers. • **Physical accessibility**: service desk locations, lighting, collection arrangement, aisle layout, signage and maps to enhance physical accessibility; turn-around time from storage facility.	• **Library strategic plan:** ➤ increase number of computers in library to improve access ➤ provide standard configuration to satisfy course requirements • **Comparison with peers:** Suggested Points of Comparison-Input Measures, Evaluation Question #6. • **User surveys & focus groups** • **Physical accessibility** study, task force report
See page 6 for complete citations.		

Access

Evaluation Questions (Extract from the Standards)
This section consists of nine questions from the Standards, and applicable checklists that you may want to consider as you review your library's access services, and assess quality of service. Use these checklists as a guide for identifying items to include in your response.

1. What <u>methods</u> are used to provide maximum <u>intellectual</u> and <u>physical accessibility</u> to the library and its resources?

Intellectual access: Briefly describe key library catalog and database search features, and how you make full use of these features.

Physical accessibility: Briefly describe how the arrangement of collections, location of service desks, the layout of aisles, lighting, and the use of signage and maps enhance physical accessibility.

2. How are the accuracy and currency of the catalog assured?

Briefly describe methods: user comments, periodic review, item status changes, and record linking to name a few.

3. Is the arrangement of the collections logical and understandable?

Briefly describe the arrangement of collections, location of service desks, and the use of signage and maps.

4. Does the library provide timely and effective interlibrary loan or document delivery service for materials not owned by the library?

In responding to this question, review participant satisfaction/service quality ratings of interlibrary loan/document delivery, and perform calculations using the following *Suggested Points of comparison: Output measures* –

- Ratio of interlibrary loan requests to combined student and faculty FTE (could be divided between photocopies and books).
- Ratio of interlibrary loan lending to borrowing.
- Interlibrary loan/document delivery borrowing turnaround time, fill rate, and unit cost.
- Interlibrary loan/document delivery lending turnaround time, fill rate, and unit cost.

Note: You may elect to omit reporting unit cost since it is a measure of efficiency.

5. Does the library participate in available consortial borrowing programs?

Briefly describe consortial borrowing programs that your institution participates in, and how these programs improve access for your users.

6. Does the library provide <u>sufficient numbers</u> of appropriately <u>capable </u>computer workstations for access to electronic resources?

In responding to this question, review participant satisfaction/service quality ratings of library computers and installed software, and perform calculations using the following *Suggested Point of comparison: Input measure –*

- Ratio of computer workstations to combined student and faculty FTE (consider that college requirements for student ownership of desktop or laptop computers could affect the need for work stations within the library).

7. Is access to the catalog and to other library resources available across campus and off-campus?

Briefly describe campus and off-campus access.

8. If materials are located in a storage facility, are those materials readily accessible?

If yes, briefly describe turnaround time.

9. In what ways does the library provide for its users who are engaged in distance learning programs?

Briefly describe access services designed for distance learners and remote users.

Worksheet for Identifying Measures of Success: Access

1. Examine your library goals and objectives. Select one that covers library access services (library catalog, circulation, reserves, consortium borrowing, interlibrary loan, document delivery, current awareness, distant learner, remote access and portal services) offered to primary clientele, library web page usability or library computer support. Write this goal or objective in the space below.

_____

_____

_____

2. Does this goal or objective support your library mission statement?   ☐ Yes ☐ No

3. Check the *purpose(s)* that this goal or objective seeks to achieve (check all that apply):

☐ improve effectiveness   ☐ improve quality   ☐ improve user satisfaction
☐ assess outcomes   ☐ monitor progress   ☐ improve efficiency
☐ educational impact   ☐ retention   ☐ placement
☐ other (please explain): _____

4. Identify *measures* that would indicate that your library has successfully achieved the above goal or objective. Selected examples include: expanded consortium and statewide efforts aimed at improving access; favorable comparison with peer libraries using suggested points of comparison (Evaluation Questions #4 and #6); positive response to web usability, service quality and user satisfaction survey questions (set % goals for each question); and replace/upgrade 25% of the library's computers annually.

_____

_____

_____

_____

5. Review your response to question 4. Have you identified at least three measures of success that can be compared over time (longitudinally) for internal analysis and/or peer group comparison? Use this space to re-write your measures as applicable.

_____

_____

_____

6. Review data sources (for examples, see performance chart, column 3) to determine what is already being collected and by who, what needs to be collected, and suggested data collection methods. Use this space for comments or questions.

_____

_____

_____

_____

User Survey Sample Questions—Access

1. How often do you use the library on weekdays, Monday through Friday?
   A. Daily/Almost Daily   B. Several times a week   C. Occasionally   D. Seldom/Never
   If you marked A or B in question 1, please skip to question 3.

2. Please indicate the reason for infrequent use of the library.
   A. My courses don't require library use.   B. I don't understand how to use library resources.
   C. I obtain needed materials elsewhere. D. Other _____

3. Do you use the library on weekends?
   A. Frequently (at least two weekends per month).
   B. Occasionally (approximately one weekend per month).
   C. Seldom or Never.

4. When are you most likely to use the library during the weekend?
   A. Saturday morning   B. Saturday afternoon   C. Saturday evening
   D. Sunday afternoon   E. Sunday night

5. Do you use the library during evening hours?
   A. Frequently (at least twice a week).
   B. Occasionally (at least once a month).
   C. Seldom or Never.

6. In general, are library hours adequate for you?   A. Yes   B. No

Please indicate your level of satisfaction by selecting one of the following choices [strongly agree **(SA)**, agree **(A)**, neutral **(N)**, disagree **(D)**, strongly disagree **(SD)**, and not applicable **(NA)**] to describe whether the following items are generally satisfactory for meeting your course needs.

	SA	A	N	D	SD	NA
7. Sufficient # of library computers and software to do your work						
8. Library catalog for locating library resources						
9. Online databases for locating academic resources and other information for your course requirements						
10. Library Web Page for accessing library services, research guides, pathfinders, catalog and journal databases						
11. Library Virtual Tour for learning about the library						

Chapter 8
STAFF

Contents:

- ➤ Essential ideas for defining and measuring your library's contribution to institutional goals
- ➤ Principles, performance areas and data sources
- ➤ Evaluation questions, including points of comparison
- ➤ Worksheet for identifying measures of success

Key Themes:

- ➤ Assessment planning begins with a review of the library mission statement in relation to the institution mission as part of the institution's strategic planning process

- ➤ Assessment of library staffing is a continuing process using a variety of methods to evaluate the following:
  - *Professional and support staff expertise in meeting current and projected program and service requirements*
  - *The role of student assistants in augmenting library staff*
  - *Capability of in-service training (for professionals – to include instructor development, for support staff, and for student assistants) to keep pace with information literacy and information technology needs in support of the curriculum*
  - *Accomplishment of institutional objectives as a result of individual participation and contributions of professionals and support staff in institutional and professional activities, publication, grant writing, and community service*
  - *Consistency of library policy with the ACRL Standards for Faculty Status for College and University Librarians*

- ➤ Link the assessment of staffing and staff contributions to the library's attainment of its mission.

Staff

Essential Ideas for Defining and Measuring Your Library's Contributions to Institutional Goals

Review the performance chart (next page) in relation to your library's goals for staff, and begin mapping this information to your institutional goals and library mission statement. As explained in Part I, it is the responsibility of the library to define and describe how its goals, objectives and intended outcomes contribute to institutional goals. Accordingly, this section addresses the need for academic libraries to develop and use measures that assess and document the contribution/ impact of the library's professional and support staff from an institutional perspective–student learning outcomes; faculty development, research and publication; and the teaching/learning environment.

Practical Solution: Develop assessment criteria and procedures for generating evidence of progress toward and/or achievement of the library's staff goals as part of the library assessment plan.

Example Library Goals	**Sample Measures of Success**[1] [illustration purposes]
Organize/maintain viable training and development practices/programs to assist staff to work effectively in a changing environment	Staff satisfaction [professional librarians and support staff] with library/institution training, and opportunities to attend professional development conferences, seminars and workshops[2]
Librarians will be active partners with classroom faculty in the academic life of the institution	Participation in faculty senate, committees, and other activities and organizations [as appropriate and depending upon qualifications and needs]
Identify faculty research interests to facilitate access to information and to enhance opportunities for publication and co-authorship	Substantive/significant linkage of library staff activities to faculty research and publication; Increase in the number of librarian and classroom faculty collaborations resulting in publication[3]

Notes:

[1] Measures of success are defined as quality, effectiveness, performance and user satisfaction/ perception measures that can be used by academic librarians to develop a culture of evidence documenting the library's contributions to institutional goals. Using section materials, develop additional measures of success to support your library's goals.

[2] Periodically survey staff concerning training and professional development needs, and their satisfaction with library, institution and other training available to staff. Excelling as a learning organization will provide libraries the capability to provide new and enhanced services that better meet user needs. Consequently, each position vacancy is a potential opportunity to re-assess skills required of new personnel.

[3] Will vary by discipline. An institutional emphasis on scholarship of teaching and assessment of student learning will support collaboration in these areas. Librarian participation in new faculty orientation provides an excellent venue for introducing services and liaison activities.

STAFF

ACRL/CLS, *Standards 2000* (Excerpt)	Performance Areas & Selected Measures	Data Sources & Applications
• The **staff** should be sufficient in <u>size</u> and <u>quantity</u> to meet the <u>programmatic</u> and <u>service needs</u> of its <u>primary users</u>. • **Librarians**, including the director, should have a graduate degree from an ALA-accredited program. . . , there may be other professional staff who will have appropriate training, experience or degrees. • **Professional library staff** should be covered by a <u>written policy</u> that clearly establishes their <u>status, rights and responsibilities</u>. This **policy** should be consistent with *ACRL Standards for Faculty Status for College and University Librarians.*	• Staff size relative to library goals and services, college programs, degrees, enrollment, size of faculty and college support staff, and auxiliary programs. Library staff size approximates or falls short of "expected" FTE size: ➢ Internal longitudinal comparison ➢ Peer comparison using FTE data [Take into account organization differences, such as centralized/decentralized technical services), library open hours, number of hours Reference/Help Desks are manned by professionals & others]	• **Library annual report** • **Library program review** • **ACRL and IPEDS data** (when possible) for comparison with peers using Suggested Points of Comparison-Input Measures, Evaluation Question #5 • **Staffing recommendations:** - self study and accreditation reports by regional and professional organizations
	• **Comparison** of library policy governing professional staff status with ACRL document: ➢ identify inconsistencies ➢ actions to resolve differences	• Copy of **library policy** covering the status of professional library staff
• **All library professionals** should be responsible for and participate in <u>professional activities</u>. • The **support staff** and **student assistants** should be assigned responsibilities appropriate to their qualifications, training, experience, and capabilities.	• **Library staff contribution**s to institutional, professional and community activities & outcomes: campus and college committees, such as undergraduate, graduate and technology committees; national, regional and state library committees; courses, workshops and separate sessions taught; publications and research guides; professional presentations; fund raising, grants, and research; and community service	• **Library annual report,** curriculum vitae, performance evaluations, and report of faculty publications: copies of material authored/co-authored by library staff, copies of publicity, such as brochures, announcements, conference programs, and web page printouts; copies of awards; and summaries of presentation evaluations and recognition letters
• The **further development** of professional and support staff should be promoted through . . . <u>continuing education</u> . . .	• Periodic **review** of staff qualifications and assignments • **Workshops**, seminars and training completed by staff	• **Staff records** • **Library strategic plan**: identify training needs and opportunities for training
See page 6 for complete citations.		

Staff

Evaluation Questions (Extract from the Standards)
This section consists of eight questions from the Standards, and applicable checklists that you may want to consider as you review your library's staffing requirements, assess training needs, and policy considerations. Use these checklists as a guide for identifying items to include in your response.

1. Does the library employ staff capable of supporting and delivering information in all available formats, including electronic resources?

Include user survey and focus group data pertaining to service points: circulation desk, reference desk, and other areas where users may receive assistance.

2. Is sufficient budgetary support provided to ensure the ongoing training of all staff?

Briefly describe funding and staff time identified for ongoing training– continuing education, staff development, and in-service training.

3. Does the library have qualified librarians, other professional staff, skilled support staff, and student assistants in adequate numbers to meet its needs?

Briefly describe staffing and qualifications by department– professional librarians, support staff and students, and identify shortfalls.

4. How does the college ensure that the library's professional staff have the appropriate accredited degrees, and how does it encourage them to engage in appropriate professional activities?

Briefly identify employment qualifications for librarians, and institution support of professional activities.

5. How does the size of the library staff relate to the goals and services of the library, the college's programs, degrees, enrollment, size of the faculty and staff, and auxiliary programs?

Briefly describe any changes in staffing that have occurred as a result of these relationships.

Suggested Points of comparison: Input measures for longitudinal analysis and comparison with peers:

- Percent of total library budget expended on staff (including the head librarian, full and part-time staff, and student assistant expenditures — including federal contributions, if any, and outsourcing costs). When determining staff expenditures care should be taken to consider comparable staff (i.e., including or excluding media, systems or development staff) and fringe benefits (within or outside the library budget).

• Ratio of FTE library staff to combined student and faculty FTE.

6. How do library staff policies and procedures compare with college guidelines and sound personnel management, especially in the areas of hiring, recruitment, appointment, contract renewal, promotion, tenure, dismissal and appeal?

Provide a brief comparison, and describe recent changes.

7. How do staff members who are responsible for instruction maintain sufficient knowledge and skills to be effective instructors?

Briefly describe instructor staff development.

8. How does the library provide security, preservation, and emergency training for its staff?

Briefly described how training is accomplished.

Worksheet for Identifying Measures of Success: Staff

1. Examine your library goals and objectives. Select one that covers staffing (size, expertise, development requirements, library policy on professional staff status or library staff contributions to institutional, professional and community activities and outcomes). Write this goal or objective in the space below.

_____

_____

_____

2. Does this goal or objective support your library mission statement? ☐ Yes ☐ No

3. Check the *purpose(s)* that this goal or objective seeks to achieve (check all that apply):

☐ improve effectiveness   ☐ improve quality   ☐ improve user satisfaction
☐ assess outcomes   ☐ monitor progress   ☐ improve efficiency
☐ educational impact   ☐ retention   ☐ placement
☐ other (please explain): _____

4. Identify *measures* that would indicate that your library has successfully achieved the above goal or objective. Selected examples include: library staff size approximates "expected" size and per cent of total library budget expended on staff approximates "expected" percentage or the library ranks in top 1/3 or top half of its peer group (using suggested points of comparison, Evaluation Question #5); and positive response to focus group, service quality and user satisfaction survey questions on service point staffing (set % goals for each question); and library staff contributions exceed requirements.

_____

_____

_____

_____

5. Review your response to question 4. Have you identified at least three measures of success that can be compared over time (longitudinally) for internal analysis and/or peer group comparison? Use this space to re-write your measures as applicable.

_____

_____

_____

6. Review data sources (for examples, see performance chart, column 3) to determine what is already being collected and by who, what needs to be collected, and suggested data collection methods. An often overlooked tool is the self assessment to determine both individual staff and group development needs that can be satisfied by library sponsored training. Use this space for comments or questions.

_____

_____

_____

_____

_____

Chapter 9
FACILITIES

Contents:

> ➤ Essential ideas for defining and measuring your library's contribution to institutional goals
> ➤ Principles, performance areas and data sources
> ➤ Evaluation questions, including points of comparison
> ➤ Worksheet for identifying measures of success
> ➤ User survey sample questions

Key Themes:

> ➤ Assessment planning begins with a review of the library mission statement in relation to the institution mission as part of the institution's strategic planning process

> ➤ Assessment of library facilities is a continuing process using a variety of methods to evaluate the accomplishment of campus-wide objectives pertaining to the following:
> • *Current and projected program and service requirements in relation to library facilities readiness –*
>   — *capacity assessment (need for a new building or expansion);*
>   — *condition assessment (need for renovation and maintenance);*
>   — *telecommunications infrastructure assessment (need for new technology, supporting communications grid, and power upgrade to offer improved levels of service)*
> • *Level of use in support of the teaching/learning environment and campus events*
> • *Creation of a holistic teaching/learning environment with secure individual and group learning spaces*

> ➤ Link the assessment of services to the library's attainment of its mission.

FACILITIES

Essential Ideas for Defining and Measuring Your Library's Contributions to Institutional Goals

Review the performance chart (next page) in relation to your library's facilities goals, and begin mapping this information to your institutional goals and library mission statement. As explained in Part I, it is the responsibility of the library to define and describe how its goals, objectives and intended outcomes contribute to institutional goals. Accordingly, this section addresses the need for academic libraries to develop and use measures that assess and document the contribution/impact of the library as a facility from an institutional perspective–student learning outcomes; faculty development, research and publication; and the teaching/learning environment.

Practical Solution: Develop assessment criteria and procedures for generating evidence of progress toward and/or achievement of the library's facilities goals as part of the library assessment plan.

Example Library Goals	Sample Measures of Success[1] [illustration purposes]
Develop a library expansion plan that establishes the library as the campus Student Learning Center.	Adoption and funding of the library building (facility) proposal [supports the institution's theme of academic distinction].[2]
Maintain renewal, adaptation and catchup facility repair activities.	Sufficient funds allocated annually for facility renewal [based on repair, replacement and subsystem life-cycle costs], and facility adaptation (alteration) [based on changes in use and regulations].[3]
Establish the library as a cultural center.	Quality exhibits and well-attended receptions co-sponsored with academic departments/campus organizations.[4]

Notes:

[1] Measures of success are defined as quality, effectiveness, performance and user satisfaction/ perception measures that can be used by academic librarians to develop a culture of evidence documenting the library's contributions to institutional goals. Using section materials, develop additional measures of success to support your library's goals

[2] Based on the results of the library space needs assessment [conducted as part of the institution's strategic planning process], the library building proposal incorporates design principles that feature interactive learning environments for individual and group study, delivery of library services, support for user-owned computers, and seamless computing integrating access, media, and software applications [in support of course assignments and curriculum portfolio requirements].

[3] Sufficient funds for catchup maintenance could also be used as a measure of success.

[4] This example is dependent on the layout/furnishings of the library facility being conducive to providing exhibits and receptions, and the emphasis given to exhibits and receptions in promoting library services. A frequently overlooked asset in promoting the library as a cultural center is the library's art collection which is oftentimes on permanent display without any publicity.

FACILITIES

ACRL/CLS, *Standards 2000* (Excerpt)	Performance Areas & Selected Measures	Data Sources & Applications
• The **library facility** should be well planned [promotes study and learning]; • it should provide **secure** and **adequate space, conducive to study and research**	• Library facility relative to library goals, services, resources, student enrollment, staff size, and size of faculty and college support staff. Library facility approximates or falls short of: ➤ "expected" size ➤ "expected" number of: seats, individual work areas, such as study carrels; group study areas; rooms equipped for presentation; electronic classrooms for hands-on interactive learning & presentation capability; and connections/power for user computers (Ethernet and wireless access).	• **Library strategic plan** • **Library program review** • **Facility recommendations-** self study and accreditation reports by regional and professional organizations • **ACRL and IPEDS data** (when possible) for comparison with peers using Suggested Points of Comparison-Input Measures, Evaluation Question #3
	• Sufficient space for: ➤ library's collections ➤ staff workspace	• **Library staff survey** • **Space Utilization study**
	• Compliance with *Americans with Disabilities Act*	• Evaluation Question #10 • Review Act
	• Facilities for distance learners in accordance with *ACRL Guidelines for Distance Learning Library Services*, Fall 2000	• Evaluation Question #11 • Review *Guidelines* at **http:www.ala.org/acrl/gu-ides/** (select from menu)
• with **suitable environmental** conditions for its services, personnel, resources and collections. • The **equipment** should be adequate and functional.	• User and library staff satisfaction with the following: ➤ adequacy & variety of study areas ➤ heating and air conditioning ➤ lighting, signage, and ➤ quantity & status of printers, photocopiers, and microfilm reader/printers (computers are covered in the Access section)	• **User and library staff surveys** • Documentation on scheduled and completed **renovations**, **improvements**, and **equipment replacement**.
See page 6 for complete citations.		

Facilities

Evaluation Questions (Extract from the Standards)
This section consists of eleven questions from the Standards, and applicable checklists that you may want to consider as you review your library's facility requirements, assess its condition, and compare it with peer library facilities. Use these checklists as a guide for identifying items to include in your response.

1. Does the library provide well-planned, secure, and adequate space for users?

Briefly describe methods used to determine if library space is well-planned, secure, and adequate for users: space study, procedures and equipment used to secure facility, and non-public areas, and user surveys.

2. Are building mechanical systems properly designed and maintained to control temperature and humidity at recommended levels?

Briefly describe the functioning of building mechanical systems.

3. What are the perceptions of users regarding the provision of conducive study spaces, including a sufficient number of seats and varied types of seating?

Summarize responses from user surveys, and use the following *Suggested Points of Comparison: Input measures* – Ratio of library seating to combined student and faculty FTE, and Ratio of library space (in square feet) to combined student and faculty FTE.
Report rank order of your library within peer group.

4. Is there enough space for the library's collections?

Briefly describe your library's space utilization and projected need.

5. Does the staff have sufficient workspace, and is it configured to promote efficient operations?

Conduct a staff workspace study and summarize results.

6. If there are branch libraries, do they have sufficient space for the collections and staff?

7. Is the library's signage adequate?

Conduct a signage study, and summarize results.

8. Does the library provide ergonomic workstations for its users and staff?

9. Are electrical and network wiring sufficient to meet the needs associated with electronic access?

Conduct study as part of library renovation and campus technology enhancement to increase the number of computers for instructional and student use.

10. Does the library meet the requirements of the Americans with Disabilities Act?

Familiar items include wheel chair/scooter accessible entrance, ADA restroom, public elevator (ramp) if multi-story building, accessible computers, and special software for vision impaired users. For extensive checklists covering all aspects of ADA Accessibility, refer to chapter 5 of the *Checklist of Library Building Design Considerations* published by ALA. Also, review state and local codes and regulations.

11. Are facilities provided to distance learners in accordance with the ACRL guidelines?
Excerpts from the Facilities Section of the ACRL *Guidelines for Distance Learning Library Services*, Fall 2000, http://www.ala.org/acrl/guides/distlrng.html –
Examples of suitable arrangements include, but are not limited to:

1. access to facilities through agreements with a non-affiliated library;
2. designated space for consultations, ready reference collections, reserve collections, electronic transmission of information, computerized database searching and interlibrary loan services, and offices for the library distance learning personnel;
3. a branch or satellite library; and
4. virtual services, such as Web pages, Internet searching, using technology for electronic connectivity.

Worksheet for Identifying Measures of Success: Facilities

1. Examine your library goals and objectives. Select one that covers library program and service needs in relation to facilities (adequate size, sufficient and secure space conducive to individual and group study/research, sufficient space for the library's collections, interactive group instruction and staff work areas, suitable environmental conditions, and adequate and functional equipment). Write this goal or objective in the space below.

_____

_____

_____

2. Does this goal or objective support your library mission statement?   ☐ Yes ☐ No

3. Check the *purpose(s)* that this goal or objective seeks to achieve (check all that apply):

☐ improve effectiveness   ☐ improve quality   ☐ improve user satisfaction
☐ assess outcomes   ☐ monitor progress   ☐ improve efficiency
☐ educational impact   ☐ retention   ☐ placement
☐ other (please explain): _____

4. Identify *measures* that would indicate that your library has successfully achieved the above goal or objective. Selected examples include: facility size and number of seats approximates "expected" size and number of seats or the library ranks in top 1/3 or top half of its peer group (using suggested points of comparison, Evaluation Question #3); positive response to focus group, service quality and user satisfaction survey questions (set % goals for each question); and compliance with the *Americans with Disabilities Act*.

_____

_____

_____

_____

5. Review your response to question 4. Have you identified at least three measures of success that can be compared over time (longitudinally) for internal analysis and/or peer group comparison? Use this space to re-write your measures as applicable.

_____

_____

_____

Standards and Assessment for Academic Libraries: A Workbook

6. Review data sources (for examples, see performance chart, column 3) to determine what is already being collected and by who, what needs to be collected, and suggested data collection methods.

_____

_____

_____

_____

_____

User Survey Sample Questions—Facilities

Please indicate your level of satisfaction by selecting one of the following choices [strongly agree **(SA)**, agree **(A)**, neutral **(N)**, disagree **(D)**, strongly disagree **(SD)**, and not applicable (NA)] to describe whether the following items are generally satisfactory for your needs:

	SA	A	N	D	SD	NA
1. General arrangement of shelving and library resources						
2. Lighting						
3. Air conditioning/heating						
4. Microfilm and microfiche reader/printer services						
5. Photocopiers						
6. Seating						
7. Private study areas						
8. Group study areas						
9. Lounge areas						

Standards and Assessment for Academic Libraries: A Workbook

Part III: Overview
Communication and Cooperation, Administration, and Budget

Introduction
This part of the workbook consists of three sections. These sections all have assessment elements in common. Evaluation questions for all three areas have basically compliance issues, i.e., the library is either doing them, or not. The academic library evaluator should, at a minimum, answer the questions from the standards. The library should ensure compliance with specific accreditation requirements, both of the regional accreditation association and specialized accreditation agencies, as appropriate for the institution. Peer comparison can be used to demonstrate the **level** of compliance.

Section Organization and Description
Each section begins with a 3-column chart to depict the relationship among library principles, performance areas, and data sources. Key principles promulgated in the *Standards* (column 1) provide the framework for identifying corresponding and related performance areas (column 2) coupled to their data sources, tools and suggested points of comparison (column 3).

Chapter 10
COMMUNICATION & COOPERATION

Contents:

> ➤ Performance chart
> ➤ Evaluation Questions

Key Themes:

> ➤ Evaluation questions for this area deal primarily with accreditation compliance issues.

> ➤ Peer comparison can be used to determine the <u>level</u> of compliance.

> ➤ Ensure compliance with specific accreditation requirements for communication and cooperation within the library and with units external to the library.

> ➤ It is critical that there be communication and cooperation between the library and information technology staffs for providing access to electronic information resources.

COMMUNICATION AND COOPERATION

ACRL/CLS, *Standards* 2000 (Excerpt)	Performance Areas & Selected Measures	Data Sources & Applications
• **Communication is essential** to ensure the smooth operation of the library. [internal] • The library should have a **regular mechanism** to communicate with the campus. [external] • Library staff should work cooperatively with **other departments** on campus. • A **special relationship** ... between the library and information technology (IT) staff in providing access to electronic information resources.	• Answer the Communication & Cooperation section questions from the ACRL Standards. • **Identify initiatives** and ongoing actions/activities pertinent to your response. • **Identify outreach opportunities** to include proposed and ongoing projects, as well as, requests for funding not already identified above. • **Analyze information** obtained from institution documents, library annual reports, policies, and practices.	• Obtain information from the following: ➢ Institutional documents ➢ Information Technology documents ➢ Library annual reports, policies, and practices ➢ Regional accreditation association standards (See Appendices) ➢ Specialized accreditation association standards (as appropriate to the institution)
• Important that library and IT **work cooperatively** and keep each other fully informed: ➢ Library usually responsible for <u>selecting and providing content</u>. ➢ IT usually provides <u>technical infrastructure</u>.	• **Examine** the working relationship between the library and information technology (IT). ➢ **Seek solutions** to any problems between the library and IT which interfere with the provision of access to electronic information resources for the campus. • **Comply with** specific requirements of accreditation associations (regional & specialized).	
See page 6 for complete citations.		

Communication and Cooperation

Evaluation Questions (Extract from the Standards)
This section includes the eight questions from the Standards. Most are questions regarding compliance–is the library actually doing this, or not. A brief explanation should be entered for those questions which can be answered affirmatively. Where the library does not comply, additional effort will be required to accurately identify the problems and seek solutions.

Immediate resolution should be sought for any problems between the library and information technology which interfere with the provision of access to electronic information resources for the campus.

1. Is there effective communication within the library that allows for a free flow of administrative and managerial information?

2. Are staff members encouraged to suggest new ideas or procedures to improve operations or working conditions within the library? Is there a process to facilitate this?

3. Does the library have a regular means to exchange information with the campus?

4. Has the library established cooperative working relationships with other departments on campus?

5. If the library and information technology are administered separately, does the organizational structure provide opportunities for productive communication and collaboration?

6. If one administrator has responsibility for both the library and information technology, how well have the two functions been integrated?

7. Is the library able to obtain technical support for information technology in the form of in-house expertise to provide electronic resources to on-site and remote users?

8. Is the capacity of the campus network sufficient to provide reasonable response times for local and remote information resources?

Chapter 11
ADMINISTRATION

Contents:

➢ Performance chart
➢ Evaluation questions

Key Themes:

➢ Evaluation questions for this area deal primarily with accreditation compliance issues.

➢ Ensure compliance with specific accreditation requirements for administration.

➢ The library should be administered in a manner that provides:
  • *Effective use of available library resources*
  • *A standing library advisory committee*
  • *Proper administration of any branch libraries*
  • *Adequate provision for distance learner services (in accordance with the ACRL Guidelines for Distance Learning Library Services)*

ADMINISTRATION

ACRL/CLS, *Standards* 2000 (Excerpt)	Performance Areas & Selected Measures	Data Sources
• The library should be administered in a manner that permits and encourages the most **effective use of available library resources**. • The **library director should report to** the president or to the appropriate chief academic officer. • There should be a **standing library advisory committee**. • The **responsibilities and authority of the director** should be defined in writing. • Any **branch libraries**, should be administered by the library director in accordance with the ACRL Guidelines for Branch Libraries in Colleges and Universities. • Any **distance learning services** provided should be administered in accordance with the ACRL Guidelines for Distance Learning Library Services.	• Answer the Administration section questions from the ACRL standards. • **Identify initiatives** and ongoing activities pertinent to your response. • **Identify** areas of **weakness** or non-compliance. • Use information obtained from institution documents, library annual report, policies, and practices. • Use peer comparison to show <u>level</u> of compliance. • Seek approval for a standing library advisory committee, if one is not already authorized • Ensure that library advisory committee membership is representative of all appropriate segments of library users. • Seek appointment of library advisory committee members with expertise in assessment and statistics. • **Comply with** specific requirements of accreditation associations (regional & specialized).	• Obtain information from the following: ➢ Institutional documents ➢ ACRL standards & guidelines — Distance learning: **http://www.ala.org/acrl/guides/distlrng.html** — Branch libraries: **http://www.ala.org/acrl/guides/branches.html** ➢ Library annual reports, policies, and practices ➢ Regional accreditation association standards (See Appendices) ➢ Specialized accreditation association standards (as appropriate to the institution ➢ Peer comparisons (as appropriate)
See page 6 for complete citations.		

Administration

Evaluation Questions (Extract from the Standards)
This section includes the seven questions from the Standards. Most are questions regarding compliance–is the library actually doing this, or not. A brief explanation should be entered for those questions which can be answered affirmatively. Where the library does not comply, additional effort will be required to accurately identify the problems and seek solutions.

The effective use of library resources is a key question for library assessment. The answer should be carefully considered and completely documented. A standing library advisory committee is a requirement for many accrediting associations and agencies.

1. How does the library administration encourage effective use of available library resources?

Determine effectiveness of procedures for the use of library resources. Use specific measures that are identified in the first nine sections of this workbook.

2. What is the statutory or legal foundation (e.g., college bylaws) for the library's activities?

3. To whom does the library director report? Is that reporting relationship appropriate?

4. Is there a document that defines the responsibilities and authority of the library director?

5. Does the library have a standing advisory committee? Does the committee have adequate classroom faculty and student representation? How effective is the committee?

An effective standing library advisory committee is very desirable, even if not required by accreditation standards. Such a committee can be of great assistance to the library as it evaluates its resources and services. Appointment of persons with expertise in surveys, statistics, and similar fields to the committee can expedite the library assessment process and provide validity and credibility to data that is collected or generated.

6. How effective are the policies and procedures that determine internal library governance and operations?

7. Does the library operate in accord with the spirit of the ALA "Library Bill of Rights"?

Chapter 12
BUDGET

Contents:

> Performance chart
> Evaluation questions, including points of comparison

Key Themes:

> Evaluation questions for this area deal primarily with accreditation compliance issues.

> Peer comparison can be used to determine the <u>level</u> of compliance.

> Ensure compliance with specific accreditation requirements for budget.

> The library should utilize its financial resources efficiently and effectively.

> The library budget should support:
> - *Appropriate library objectives*
> - *Reasonable expectations of library users*
> - *Appropriate levels of staffing*
> - *Adequate staff compensation*

BUDGET

ACRL/CLS, *Standards 2000* (Excerpt)	Performance Areas & Selected Measures	Data Sources & Applications
• The **library director should** <u>prepare</u>, <u>justify</u>, **and** <u>administer</u> **a library budget** that is appropriate to the library's objectives. • The budget should **meet the reasonable expectations of library users** when balanced against other college needs. • The library should **utilize its financial resources** efficiently and effectively. • The **library director should have authority to apportion funds and initiate expenditures** within the library budget and in accordance with college policy. • The budget should **support appropriate levels of staffing** and adequate <u>staff compensation.</u>	• Library budget approximates or falls short of "expected" budget. ➢ **Apply multiple regression analysis** to peer data to determine how own library budget compares to that "expected," based on multiple data elements. • Answer the Budget section questions from the ACRL Standards. • **Identify initiatives** and ongoing actions pertinent to your response. ➢ **Comply with** specific requirements of accreditation associations (regional & specialized) • **Identify** areas of **weakness** or non-compliance. ➢ **Record and analyze** library & peer comparison data· Use peer comparison to show level of compliance • Use peer comparison to show <u>level</u> of compliance	• Obtain information from the following: ➢ Institutional documents ➢ Longitudinal data (internal trends) ➢ Peer comparisons — ACRL — IPEDS — Selected peer groups ➢ Studies and reports ➢ Library annual reports, policies, and practices ➢ Regional accreditation association standards (See Appendices) ➢ Specialized accreditation association standards (as appropriate to the institution)
See page 6 for complete citations.		

Budget

Evaluation Questions (Extract from the Standards)
This section includes the twelve questions from the Standards. Most are questions regarding compliance–is the library actually doing this, or not. A brief explanation should be entered for those questions which can be answered affirmatively. Where the library does not comply, additional effort will be required to accurately identify the problems and seek solutions.

The availability and effective use of library funds is a key question for library assessment. Peer comparison can be used to help determine the availability of adequate funds for similar academic libraries, but care should be taken to insure that the data used are comparable.

Although comparison of the percentage of institutional E & G (educational and general) expenditures among libraries is **not** recommended, helpful information can be obtained by calculating the institutional E & G expenditures for a single academic library, over time. If, for example, the library percentage declined over a given period of time, it can be inferred that the library is not receiving the same share of the institutional expenditures. Such a calculation allows for a fair comparison of annual library expenditures, especially during periods of rapid change or fluctuation in the amount of institutional expenditures.

1. Does the library director prepare, justify, and administer the library budget in accordance with agreed upon objectives?

Library goals and objectives should be compatible with the institutional mission (see planning section) and should be approved by the appropriate institutional authorities.

2. Are the library's annual authorized expenditures adequate to meet the ongoing, appropriate needs of the library?

Use peer comparison from a special data collection effort (own peer group, for example) or from other data sources as defined in the first three sections of this handbook. Opinion surveys of key library users can be used to collect information regarding these users' perceptions of whether or not the appropriate needs of the library are being met.

3. How is the college's curriculum taken into account when formulating the library's budget?

Ensure that all new or expanded programs or courses include an institutional assessment (including library input) of the need for new or expanded library resources to support such offerings.

4. How are the instructional methods of the college, especially as they relate to independent study, considered when formulating the library's budget?

5. What methods are used to determine the adequacy of existing collections? Is the budget adequate to maintain an appropriate rate of collection development in fields pertinent to the curriculum?

6. How does the size, or anticipated size, of the student body and the classroom faculty affect the library budget?

7. Does the budget support an appropriate level of staffing and compensation?

Use peer comparison from a special data collection effort (own peer group, for example) or from other data sources as defined in the first three sections of this handbook.

8. How is the adequacy and availability of funding for other library resources (e.g., Archives and Special Collections) determined?

9. Does the library budget reflect the library's responsibility for acquiring, processing, servicing, and providing access to media and computer resources?

10. To what extent does the library director have authority to apportion funds and initiate expenditures within the library budget and in accordance with college policy?

11. How does the library monitor its encumbrances and the payment of its invoices? How does the library determine its choices and schedule its expenditures?

Standard accounting methods and practices should be used in ordering and making payment for library materials and services. An approved collection development policy should be in place and reviewed regularly to ensure that current institutional priorities are addressed.

12. Does the budget include adequate support for extended campus programs?

Library services for extended campus programs and distance learning programs must be equivalent to those provided to library users on the main campus. Apply the ACRL Guidelines for Distance Learning Library Services, as appropriate.

Suggested Points of Comparison: Input measures
Use peer comparison from a special data collection effort (own peer group, for example) or from other data sources as defined in the first three sections of this handbook.

- Ratio of material/information resource expenditures to combined total student and faculty FTE.

➢ Percent of total library budget expended in the following three categories:

1. materials/information resources, subdivided by print, microform, and electronic.

2. staff (including the head librarian, full and part-time staff, and student assistant expenditures - including federal contributions, if any, and outsourcing costs). When determining staff expenditures care should be taken to consider comparable staff (i.e., including or excluding media, systems or development staff) and fringe benefits (within or outside the library budget).

3. all other operating expenses (care should be taken to include the same categories, e.g., network infrastructure, equipment).

Regional Accreditation Association Standards: CITATIONS & Current Status

The intent of reprinting selected information is to display the inter-relationship of these documents with the ACRL *College Library Standards, 2000 edition*, and to identify measures one can use to demonstrate continuing improvement. The editors thank the six regional accrediting associations, copyright holders of the excerpted material used in these charts. Please refer to the complete documents listed below for accreditation purposes.

Appendix

D-1. *Characteristics of Excellence in Higher Education*, 1994 ed. Commission on Higher Education, Middle States Association of Colleges and Schools. Philadelphia: 1994. **http://www.msache.org/msachar.pdf** [last accessed 7-1-2002]

The current standard; effective through 2002-2003.

D-2. 2002 ed. **http://www.msache.org/charac02.pdf** [last accessed 7-1-2002]

Standard adopted January 2002; effective in 2003-2004.

E. *Handbook of Accreditation*, 2nd ed. North Central Association of Colleges and Schools, Commission on Institutions of Higher Education. Chicago: 1997 & March 2000 *Addendum* & February 2002 revision (from Web site). **http://www.ncahigherlearningcommission.org/resources/policies/edinstia.html#1a** [last accessed 7-1-2002]

Proposed new Criteria for Accreditation available at: **http://www.ncahigherlearningcommission.org/restructuring/newcriteria/index.html#supplemental** [last accessed 7-1-2002]

The new standard will not be effective until after September 2004.

F. *Standards for Accreditation*, 2001 ed. New England Association of Schools and Colleges, Commission on Institutions of Higher Education. Bedford, MA: 1992 & 2001. **http://www.neasc.org/cihe/stancihe.htm** [last accessed 7-1-2002]

Standards adopted in 1992 and revised in 2001.

G. *Accreditation Handbook*, 1999 ed. Northwest Association of Schools and Colleges, Commission on Colleges. Bellevue, WA: 1999. **http://www.cocnasc.org/** [click on "standards" at left of screen.] [last accessed 7-1-2002]

H-1. *Criteria for Accreditation*. Southern Association of Colleges and Schools, Commission on Colleges. Decatur, GA: 2000 [1997, Eleventh ed., Second printing]. **http://www.sacscoc.org/criteria.asp** [last accessed 7-1-2002]

The current standard; effective through 2003.

H-2. *Principles of Accreditation: Foundations for Quality Enhancement*. Southern Association of Colleges and Schools, Commission on Colleges. [Decatur, GA: 2001]. **http://www.sacscoc.org/accrrevproj.asp** [last accessed 7-1-2002]

Standard adopted December 2001; effective in 2004.

I. *WASC Handbook of Accreditation/2001*. Western Association of Schools & Colleges, Senior College Commission. Alameda, CA: 2001. **http://www.wascweb.org/senior/handbook.pdf** [last accessed 7-1-2002]

These new standards were adopted in 2001.

Appendix A
Selected Bibliography on Academic Library Assessment

ACRL. *Information Literacy Competency Standards for Higher Education.*
http://www.ala.org/acrl/ilcomstan.html

These standards were approved in January 2000. ACRL seeks endorsement and promulgation of these standards from professional and accreditation associations in higher education. An Information Literacy Standards Implementation Task Force is charged with promoting the use of these standards in higher education.

ACRL. *Sources of Information on Performance and Outcomes Assessment.*
http://www.ala.org/acrl/sacguid.html

A 44-item annotated bibliography prepared by the ACRL Standards and Accreditation Committee in 1997.

ACRL. "Standards for College Libraries, The Final Version, approved January 2000." *C&RL News*, March 2000, 61:175-82. **http://www.ala.org/acrl/guides/college.html**

The first edition of the Standards for College Libraries was published in 1959. Subsequent editions were published in 1975, 1986, and 1995. The standards are the responsibility of the College Libraries Section Standards Committee, a standing committee of the College Libraries Section of ACRL.

The CLS Standards Committee encouraged review of the new draft standards by as many people as possible. The Committee published the draft standards in the May 1999 issue of *C&RL News*; held a public hearing at the New Orleans Annual Meeting of ALA in July 1999; posted the draft standards on the ACRL web-site; solicited feedback on listservs; and published an article on the draft standards in the *CLS Newsletter*.

ACRL. *Task Force on Academic Library Outcomes Assessment Report*, June 27, 1998.
http://www.ala.org/acrl/outcome.html

About 20 years ago higher education began to focus on measuring the outcomes of its programs as the primary indicator of quality. A primary force that impelled this focus included a restructuring of the criteria of the regional accrediting agencies to emphasize assessment; also, virtually every state higher education coordinating board now requires public institutions to annually provide accountability data in terms of output measures.

The formation of the Task Force was a response to the ACRL Board's perception that the association had no statement on outcomes assessment, and that its standards, largely written as input measures, were out of step with the practices and philosophy of regional and professional accrediting agencies and state higher education agencies.

The Task Force was given three charges: (1) Develop a philosophical framework for assessing libraries in terms of desired campus outcomes; (2) Develop prototypes for such assessment;

and (3) Develop a recommendation for one or more processes for implementation of the former [#2] with a time frame for completion.

The apparent conflict between input standards on the one hand and the trends towards greater attention to outcomes as a method of assessment has been a profession-wide concern as evidenced by the many articles in the literature. This Task Force report therefore includes suggestions for incorporating outcomes assessment into ACRL standards, as well as for using them in other contexts. The document also provides useful definitions for the terms: "outcomes," "inputs," and "standards."

ARL. *A Bimonthly Report on Research Library Issues and Actions from ARL, CNI, and SPARC.* **http://www.arl.org/newsltr/index.html** Click "Measurements of Research Libraries" (left frame) for recent articles.

This publication from ARL (Association of Research Libraries), CNI (Coalition of Networked Information), and SPARC (Scholarly Publishing and Academic Resources Coalition), reports on current issues of interest to academic and research library administrators, staff, and users; and others in higher education. Each issue explores a broad range of education topics of particular importance to research institutions and academic librarians.

Burkhardt, Joanna, and Lisabeth Chabot. *Bibliography for Evaluation/Assessment.* June 2000. **http://abell.austinc.edu/CLS/bibliography.html**

A 40-item bibliography compiled by the College Library Section, Continuing Education Committee to accompany the introduction of the 2000 edition of the Standards for College Libraries.

Butler University Libraries. [2002] "Accreditation Self-Study." **http://www.butler.edu/library/selfstudy.pdf**

Using the framework of the ACRL College Library Standards 2000 edition, this self-study was completed in 2002, in preparation for a 2002-2003 institutional review by the North Central Association.

Governors State University Library. [2000] "GSU Implementation of Standards for College Libraries, 2000 edition." **http://www.govst.edu/library/assess.htm**

GSU was the first library to apply the complete College Library Standards, 2000 edition and make them available on the web. Becky Bostian was at that time library director, and a member of the CLS Standards Committee, which wrote the standards. GSU used the final draft and had the document ready in January 2000, the month the Standards were officially approved.

Gratch-Lindauer, Bonnie. *Assessment Methods by Learning Domains With Examples.* CARL Conference, Community College Program on Information Competency, October 10-12, 1999 (updated 8/2001). **http://fog.ccsf.cc.ca.us/~bgratch/CARLhandouts.html**

Excellent list of 20+ examples of library and information literacy assessment methods practiced in higher education. Examples are grouped into one of the following learning domains: affective, behavioral and cognitive learning. Links updated annually.

————. "Comparing the Regional Accreditation Standards: Outcomes Assessment and Other Trends," *The Journal of Academic Librarianship*, January–March 2002, 28:14–25.

Bonnie's thorough comparison and analysis of the regional accreditation standards and her findings and recommendations provide a much needed strategy for academic libraries to be active partners in assessing student needs and outcomes.

————. "Defining and Measuring the Library's Impact on Campuswide Outcomes," *College & Research Libraries*, November 1998, 59: 546-570.

An attribute to her leadership in the field of library assessment, this seminal article earned Bonnie the ACRL Instruction Section Instruction Publication of the Year Award in 2000. The article provides a methodology for assessing the library's impact on key institutional outcomes to which academic libraries contribute. Five checklists, labeled as figures, make the content actionable, and a must read for academic librarians involved in implementing outcomes assessment. Extensive footnotes document the literature review.

————. *Measuring What Matters: A Library/LRC Outcomes Assessment Manual*. Fairfield, CA: Learning Resources Association of California Community Colleges, 2000.

Published as a loose-leaf handbook with reproducible worksheets, this guide uses a six-step approach (acronym ADICAC for align, define, identify, chart/collect, analyze and communicate) to the outcomes assessment process.

Hernon, Peter and Robert E. Dugan. *Action Plan for Outcomes Assessment in Your Library*. Chicago: ALA, 2002.

This publication addresses the need for academic librarians to become conversant with outcomes assessment by providing a plan that incorporates theory and accreditation policies, models, examples of criteria, information gathering and reporting.

————, and Ellen Altman. *Assessing Service Quality: Satisfying the Expectations of Library Customers*. Chicago: ALA, 1998.

Measuring service quality in academic and public libraries is the theme of this publication with its focus on the customer as the primary source of information. Using focus groups and surveys to collect information, librarians can select specific service quality factors they want to assess by adapting model forms provided by Hernon and Altman.

————, Danuta A. Nitecki, and Ellen Altman. "Service Quality and Customer Satisfaction: An Assessment and Future Directions," *The Journal of Academic Librarianship*, January 1999, 25: 9-17.

This article defines and applies the concepts of service quality and satisfaction to academic libraries, identifies reasons for resistance to service quality, suggests an agenda for research, and provides a literature overview with extensive footnotes.

————, and John R. Whitman. *Delivering Satisfaction and Service Quality: A Customer-Based Approach for Libraries*. Chicago: ALA, 2000.

Build loyalty to your library using proven and practical strategies presented in this ALA "Service Quality" series publication which includes questionnaires. Use the step-by-step instructions to learn how to develop a plan that is customized to your users' needs, collect and analyze your data, and report your results.

Information and Documentation–Library Performance Indicators. First Edition, ISO 11620. Geneve, Switzerland: International Organization for Standardization, 1998.

Published by the International Organization for Standardization, ISO 11620 defines a set of 29 indicators for assessing traditional library services grouped into three areas: user satisfaction, public services, and technical services.

Inter-University Consortium for Political and Social Research (ICPSR).

Located at the University of Michigan in Ann Arbor, ICPSR provides convenient access to data holdings containing 5000+ studies and 50,000+ files. These files consist mainly of raw data, and some time series. To learn more about accessing ICPSR data, membership benefits, and the role of the academic library, visit their web site at http://www.icpsr.umich.edu.

Kaplan, Robert S. and David P. Norton. *The Strategy-Focuses Organization: How Balanced Scorecard Companies Thrive in the New Business Environment*. Boston: Harvard Business School Press, 2000.

The central theme of this book is to create a strategy scorecard consisting of measurements that communicate to the organization what is important–how business units create value for current and future customers.

Kena, Jenny. *Performance Indicators for the Electronic Library*. (Updated 10/23/1999). **http:// www.ozemail.com.au/~jkena/perf.html**

The material on the website describes the "electronic library" and how performance measurement of these resources and services differs from that for the traditional library. Peter Brophy in the UK devised a framework of performance indicators for electronic resources that can potentially be used by all types of libraries. Brophy's work is described, then used to illustrate the progress in collecting and reporting performance data for such services in a group of public libraries.

Measuring Quality: International Guidelines for Performance Measurement in Academic Libraries. (IFLA Publication, v. 76) New Providence, NJ: Bowker-Saur, 1996.

This monograph is the product of an IFLA working group which evaluated the existing literature on performance measurement and drew up a list for academic libraries. They are designed to measure effectiveness not efficiency, and are concentrated on user-oriented indicators. Each included indicator is designed to assess either the quality of the library's overall performance, or the quality of a specific service or activity. The publication includes a comprehensive bibliography (37 pages) of literature dealing with performance measurement. Also included are English, French, German, Russian, and Spanish glossaries.

There is a general introduction on the need for, and use of, effective management tools in academic libraries. The discussion covers: quality, quality management, mission & goals, stakeholder approach, performance measurement, measuring outcome, and results of performance measurement. More detailed discussions are included in the chapters, "The Measurement Process" and "Cost-effectiveness."

Seventeen performance indicators are described in detail in the following seven categories: general library use and facilities, collection quality, catalog quality, availability of documents in the collection, reference services, remote use, and user satisfaction.

"Measuring Service Quality." *Library Trends* (Spring 2001). Symposium, October 20-21, 2000.

This theme issue consists of eleven articles that report on library service quality research and studies presented at the ARL October 2000 symposium annual meeting.

Recognizing that there are different perspectives and methodologies for measuring service quality, these articles cover the gamut of topics: the use of LibQual to measure the gap between clients' desired service levels and their perception of service received, the challenges of measuring service quality in a networked environment, the library as a learning organization, the use of the Balanced Scorecard adapted to academic libraries, the use of service quality assessment from a local planning perspective, and how user satisfaction relates to service quality. Preprint papers for many of these articles are accessible at **http://www.arl.org/libqual/events/oct2000msq/program.html**

NCES Library Peer Comparison Tool

The NCES has loaded the academic library peer comparison tool. Use it at: **http://nces.ed.gov/surveys/libraries/academicpeer/**

"The Academic Library Peer Comparison Tool allows users to get information on a particular library, or to customize a peer group by selecting the key variables that are used to define it. Users can then view customized reports of the comparison between the library of interest and its peers, on a variety of variables as selected by the user."

"These data have not been imputed for non-response, so some data for some libraries may be missing. This may mean that some libraries will not be selected as peers. Because public use data must protect the confidentiality of respondents, changes have been made in the public use file."

OCLC Lacy Product Center. ACAS links. http://www.wln.com/products/aca/index.htm

The website describes the Automated Collection Assessment & Analysis Services (ACAS) offered thorough OCLC, for a fee. The services include: Collection Analysis, Title Overlap Analysis, Library Collection Comparisons, List Comparison Service, and OCLC's WLN Conspectus Database Software. Information and links are provided.

"Outcomes Assessment in Higher Education," *The Journal of Academic Librarianship*, January-March, 2002, 28 (No.1 & 2) [Special Issue]

This timely special issue consists of an editorial and eight articles which develop key aspects of outcomes assessment, such as accreditation principles and the elements of assessment: inputs, activities (within processes and functions), outputs, outcomes, and expectations (service quality and user satisfaction).

Perspectives on Outcome Based Evaluation for Libraries and Museums. Institute of Museum and Library Services Publications. **http://www.imls.gov/pubs/** Click "Publications," (left frame)

This publication discusses a method of program evaluation increasingly preferred by many who fund libraries and museums. Of particular note is the article, "Documenting the Difference: Demonstrating the Value of Libraries Through Outcome Measurement," p. 16-23, by Peggy D. Rudd. She points out that besides using outcomes to better understand the effect of the library on users, program performance and results-based planning, budgeting, and public reporting are becoming the norm nationwide.

Also see the Outcome Based Evaluation section on the IMLS site.

"Perspectives on Quality in Libraries." *Library Trends* (Winter, 1996).

The ten articles published in this issue as introduced by the issue editor "represent an extraordinary set of perspectives on quality." Articles in this issue cover academic, community college and public libraries, school media centers, strategies for change, quality initiatives, and quality of public services.

Poll, Roswitha. "Performance, Processes, and Costs: Managing Service Quality with the Balanced Scorecard," *Library Trends*, Spring 2001, 49:709–717.

Reports on the use of the Balanced Scorecard (adapted to the conditions of three of Germany's largest libraries) to create a quality management system.

Proceedings of the 3rd Northumbria International Conference on Performance Measurement in Libraries and Information Services. Newcastle upon Tyne: Information North for the School of Information Studies, University of Northumbria at Newcastle, 2000.

The proceedings include 45 papers, and reflect the following themes: (1) defining and measuring values, and (2) identifying and assessing outcomes and impacts of library services–electronic library and network measurement indicators, benchmarking, scorecard models, government involvement, quality service measurements and applications, management information services, and activity based costing.

Sannwald, William W. *Checklist of Library Building Design Considerations*. 4th Edition. Chicago: ALA, 2001.

Consisting of thirteen chapters, *Checklist* with its easy to use checklist format will help you evaluate current and future needs relating to space and function design considerations including American with Disabilities Act requirements.

Wallace, Valeri E., "OVERCITES: Outcomes Assessment in Academic Libraries: Library Literature in the 1990's," *College and Undergraduate Libraries*, vol. 8, no. 2.

A forthcoming article which provides an excellent review of the literature on outcomes assessment in academic libraries in the 1990's focusing on performance measures and indicators, outcomes, and impacts. Includes a 38-item bibliography.

Appendix B

Factors That Drive Performance Are Derived from the Following:

Inputs	Output Examples
• Money	• # of Books Circulated
• Space	• # of Computers
• Online Resources	• # of Reference, Database, ILL & Reserve Transactions
• Collection	• # of Library Orientations & Bibliographic Instruction Sessions
• Staff	• # of Faculty Using Current Awareness Services
• Equipment	• # of Hours Library is Open

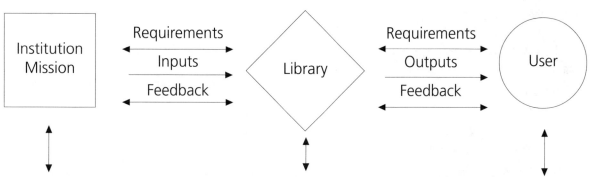

Uses of Evaluation, Assessment, and Outcomes Assessment	Processes Within These Functions	Outcome Performance Indicators
• Accreditation	• Services	• Course Research Requirements
• Appropriateness of Goals & Objectives - Effectiveness	• Instruction	• Information Literacy Competencies & Lifelong Learning Skills
• Strategic Planning	• Resources	• Discipline Competencies
• Accountability	• Access	• Impact of Library Services
• Adequacy of Inputs, Processes, Outcomes, and Service Quality	• Staff	**Service Quality Dimensions**
• Efficiency	• Facilities	• Library as a Learning Place
• Funding	• Communication and Cooperation	• Self-Empowering, Timely & Reliable Access
• Distance Learner Support	• Administration	• Tools to Complete Research Requirements
• Career Placement & Graduate School	• Budget	• Access & Collections that Keep Pace with Curriculum & Technology

Appendix C
Augusta State University–Graduating Student Survey–Spring 2000

REESE LIBRARY
Student Satisfaction Survey

Dear Student:

Reese Library seeks help in understanding the needs of students, faculty, and staff at ASU. We, the members of the library committee, have prepared a series of questions, with the intent of finding out how the library can improve its services. Please take the time to answer these questions candidly. We have enclosed a postage-paid envelope for you to return your completed survey to the Library. Your timely response is greatly appreciated. We wish you well for a bright future.

We look forward to hearing from you.

Sincerely,

Dr. William N. Nelson, Director of Reese Library
Dr. Sankar Sethuraman, Chair of Library Committee
Reese Library
Augusta State University
2500 Walton Way
Augusta GA, 30904

General information about you
1. You are graduating from ASU with
   ☐   Bachelor's degree
   ☐   Master's degree
   ☐   Associate's degree
   ☐   Specialist's degree

2. During a typical semester, you <u>primarily</u>
☐ Go to the library   ☐ Access the library on line ☐ Both

3. During a typical semester, you use the library (either by going there or by accessing it on line)
☐ Not at all   ☐ 1-10 times   ☐ 11-20 times   ☐ 21-30 times   ☐ More than 30 times

4. You most often use the library during
☐ Mornings ☐ Afternoons   ☐ Evenings   ☐ Weekends   ☐ All of these times

5. The main reason you go to the library is for

☐ Research   ☐ Study   ☐ Computing   ☐ Copying   ☐ Social or other

6. Your major is: _____

Library and Media Services

For each of the following questions, indicate your level of satisfaction by selecting one of the choices (strongly agree **(SA)**, agree **(A)**, neutral **(N)**, disagree **(D)** or strongly disagree **(SD)**) as your response. If you have not used the facility or have not received the service or the question does not apply to you, then choose N/A as your option.

	SA	A	N	D	SD	NA
7. Library hours are convenient and adequate.						
8. Media Services hours are convenient and adequate.						
9. Directional signs in the library are clear and helpful.						
10. Materials (books, journals, etc.) are in their proper places on shelves.						
11. The Library Online Catalog, ATLAS, is easy to use.						
12. GALILEO contributes to meeting my information needs.						
13. Materials requested by interlibrary loan are received within the time frame quoted.						
14. Informational brochures (subject guides, information guides on Galileo, floor plans, etc.) are easily available and helpful.						
15. The Library holds an adequate range of books needed for my major.						
16. The Library holds an adequate range of journals needed for my major.						
17. The Library holds an adequate range of magazines, newspapers, and documents needed for my major.						
18. The Library maintains an adequate range of online resources (CD ROMs, WEB) for my major.						
19. Media Services provides an adequate range of non-print materials needed for my major.						
20. The Library maintains an adequate range of resources and services specifically needed for my research.						

	SA	A	N	D	SD	NA
21. The Library provides an adequate number of study areas.						
22. The Library provides quiet study areas.						
23. The lighting in the library is adequate for my needs.						
24. The temperature in the library is comfortable.						
25. General arrangement of shelving and library resources is helpful to my needs.						
26. The Library offers an adequate number of library instruction classes.						
27. Library instruction in information and technological competencies has helped improve my research skills.						
28. The check out process for library materials is easy.						
29. The circulation period allows sufficient time for use.						
24. The Library has an effective reserve system.						
25. The Library provides useful reference service.						
26. The Library has an effective interlibrary loan system.						
27. The Library offers effective library instructional programs.						
28. Media Services provides helpful instruction with the operation of equipment.						
29. The Library provides an adequate number of computers for my research needs.						
30. The printers are generally satisfactory for my research needs.						
31. The microfilm and the microfiche reader/printers are generally satisfactory for my research needs.						
32. The photocopiers are generally satisfactory for my research needs.						
33. Equipment for users with disabilities is generally satisfactory for my research needs.						
34. I am satisfied with the nature and diversity of library-sponsored events.						
35. The Library has helped me become more proficient at using technology to find information for my needs.						

	SA	A	N	D	SD	NA
36. The Library has been instrumental in developing my interest in lifelong learning.						
37. I am generally satisfied with the collection of browsing books in the library.						

For each of the following questions on staff performance in the Library and Media Services, indicate your level of satisfaction on a scale from 1 to 5 (1 = Lowest , 5 = Highest).

Write N/A if you have not received a particular service.

	Circulation Dept.	Reserve Dept.	Reference Dept.	Inter-library Loan Dept.	Periodicals Dept.	Media Services
1. Staff are approachable and welcoming.						
2. Staff are courteous and polite.						
3. Staff are available when I need them.						
4. Staff give accurate answers to my questions.						
5. Staff encourage me to come back to ask for more assistance if I need it.						
6. Staff are sensitive to the needs of people different from themselves.						

If you have any additional comments, you may include those in the space below.

_____

_____

_____

_____

Thank you very much for completing this survey. Please place your completed survey in the enclosed self-addressed, postage-paid envelope and return it to the library.

APPENDIX D-1

Regional Accreditation Standards: Provisions Affecting Academic Libraries
(Middle States–1994; current standards)

ACRL Standards Section	Middle States Association of Colleges and Schools, Commission on Higher Education, Characteristics of Excellence in Higher Education, 1994 edition [current standards]
Planning	"The distinguishing marks of well-defined goals and objectives include the following: They are clear, expressed in simple terms appropriate to higher education and broad in scope;...They are stated in terms of results sought and the means by which they are to be attained;...They are understood and utilized within the institution as guides for thought and action. Equally important are the objectives of particular units...." p. 7-8. "Institutional goals and objectives must provide the foundation for sound institutional planning." p. 17. "One measure of an institution's integrity is its application of data generated through the assessment process to sound planning and resource allocation." p. 17.
Assessment	"Careful evaluation of all learning resources, on-site or elsewhere, should be an ongoing process." p. 16. "Provision for implementation and for evaluation of the results of planning should be built into the process." p. 18. "The plan for the assessment of outcomes should attempt to determine the extent and quality of student learning." p. 17. "Systematic procedures for evaluating administrative units and opportunities for the professional renewal of personnel should be established." p. 20. "Institutions should develop guidelines and procedures for assessing their overall effectiveness as well as student learning outcomes. The deciding factor in assessing institutional effectiveness is evidence of the extent to which it achieves its goals and objectives." p. 16.
Outcomes Assessment	"A system for assessing the effectiveness of library and learning resources should be available. It should focus on utilization, accessibility, availability, and delivery of materials. Quality and relevance of the collections, effectiveness of reference and referral services, and adequacy of funding for resources and their use are essential. Ultimately, the most important measure will be how effectively students are prepared to become independent, self-directed learners." p. 16. "Outcomes assessment involves gathering and evaluating both quantitative and qualitative data which demonstrate congruence between the institution's mission, goals, and objectives and the actual outcomes of its educational programs and activities." "An institution should be able to demonstrate that the information obtained is used as the basis for ongoing self-renewal." p. 17.

Standards and Assessment for Academic Libraries: A Workbook

APPENDIX D-1

Regional Accreditation Standards: Provisions Affecting Academic Libraries
(Middle States–1994; current standards)

ACRL Standards Section	Middle States Association of Colleges and Schools, Commission on Higher Education, Characteristics of Excellence in Higher Education, 1994 edition [current standards]
Services	"The development of services and collections must relate realistically to the institution's educational mission, goals, curricula, size, complexity, degree level, fiscal support, and its teaching, learning, and research requirements." p. 15."
	The services, resources, and programs of libraries, broadly defined, are fundamental to the educational mission of an institution and to the teaching and learning process. They support the educational program. They facilitate learning and research activities among students, faculty, and staff." p. 15.
	"Interlibrary loan services should be available, well supported, and structured to ensure timely delivery of materials." p. 16.
Instruction	A variety of contemporary technologies for accessing learning resources and instruction in their use should be available." p. 15.
	"It is essential to have an active and continuing program of library orientation and instruction in accessing information...." p. 15.
	"Each institution should foster optimal use of its learning resources through strategies designed to help students develop information literacy-the ability to locate, evaluate, and use information in order to become independent learners." p. 15.
Resources	"An institution should provide access to a broad range of learning resources, at both primary and off-campus sites." p. 15.
	"[Library/learning resources] must be in reasonable proportion to the needs to be served, but numbers alone are no assurance of excellence. Of more importance are the quality, accessibility, availability, and delivery of resources on site and elsewhere; their relevance to the institution's current programs; and the degree to which they are actually used." p. 15.
	"In institutions where graduate instruction and research constitute a major part of the overall program, recognition must be given to the extended demands placed on faculty, finances, facilities, library, and other resources." p. 14.
Access	"An institution should provide access to a broad range of learning resources, at both primary and off-campus sites. Although access to these resources is customarily gained through a library/resource center, an attempt should be made to think beyond the physical confines of the traditional library in regard to information access. A variety of contemporary technologies for accessing learning resources and instruction in their use should be available." p. 15.
	"Students, faculty, and staff should have access to remote as well as on-site information resources." p. 15.
	"Computer and other technological systems can assist in providing convenient access." p. 16.

APPENDIX D-1

Regional Accreditation Standards: Provisions Affecting Academic Libraries
(Middle States–1994; current standards)

ACRL Standards Section	Middle States Association of Colleges and Schools, Commission on Higher Education, Characteristics of Excellence in Higher Education, 1994 edition [current standards]
Staff	"All staff should work together to plan for the management, evaluation, and use of learning resources." p. 16. "Librarians, information specialists, and other staff must demonstrate their professional competence on the basis of criteria comparable to those for other faculty and staff. They should help facilitate the teaching and learning process, especially in assisting students to improve their information skills. The status of members of the library staff should be commensurate with the significance and responsibilities of their positions." p. 16
Facilities	"These common characteristics of excellence [include]...physical facilities that meet the needs of the institution's programs and functions." p. 4. "Library buildings and comparable facilities—whether on or off-campus—should be designed to provide convenient access for users. Such features as seating, lighting, arrangement of books and materials, and acoustical treatment are important and are to be judged by their effectiveness in making the facility an attractive place for study, research, and teaching. Nothing else matters if resources are not used." p. 16.
Communication & Cooperation	"It is essential to have an active and continuing program of library orientation and instruction in accessing information, developed collaboratively and supported actively by faculty, librarians, academic deans, and other information providers." p. 15. "Teaching faculty, librarians, and other information providers should collaborate on the selection of materials, based on intellectual and cultural depth and breadth." p. 16. "Communication promotes and sustains good working relations and healthy institutional morale. Continuing and systematic efforts must be devoted to maintaining the flow of essential information to and from all individuals concerned with an institution's welfare." p. 19.
Administration	"These common characteristics of excellence [include]...library and learning resources sufficient to support the programs offered and evidence of their use." p. 4. "All staff should work together to plan for the management, evaluation, and use of learning resources." p. 16. "Organization and administration are important, and their importance is measured by the degree to which they facilitate excellent teaching and successful learning." p. 19. "Administrators must be qualified to provide effective leadership and efficient management consonant with the institution's goals, objectives, size, and complexity." p. 20.

APPENDIX D-1

Regional Accreditation Standards: Provisions Affecting Academic Libraries
(Middle States–1994; current standards)

ACRL Standards Section	Middle States Association of Colleges and Schools, Commission on Higher Education, Characteristics of Excellence in Higher Education, 1994 edition [current standards]
Budget	"A sound budget accurately reflects institutional resources, needs, plans, and priorities." p. 19. "One measure of an institution's integrity is its application of data generated through the assessment process to sound planning and resource allocation." p. 17. "These common characteristics of excellence [include]... financial resources sufficient to assure the quality and continuity of the institution's programs and services." p. 4. "However, since a budget is the financial expression of an institution's plans and priorities, it should be developed through consultation with departments, divisions, and other academic and administrative units." p. 18.

APPENDIX D-2

Regional Accreditation Standards: Provisions Affecting Academic Libraries
(Middle States-2002; effective 2003-04)

ACRL Standards Section	Middle States Association of Colleges and Schools, Commission on Higher Education, Characteristics of Excellence in Higher Education, 2002 edition [Adopted January, 2002; mandatory in 2003-2004]
Planning	The institution's mission clearly defines its purpose within the context of higher education and explains whom the institution serves and what it intends to accomplish. The institution's stated goals and objectives, consistent with the aspirations and expectations of higher education, clearly specify how the institution will fulfill its mission. (Standard 1)
Assessment	The mission, goals, and objectives are developed and recognized by the institution with its members and its governing body and are utilized to develop and shape its programs and practices and to evaluate its effectiveness. (Standard 1) An institution conducts ongoing planning and resource allocation based on its mission and uses the results of its assessment activities for institutional renewal. (Standard 2) The institution has developed and implemented an assessment plan and process that evaluates its overall effectiveness in: achieving its mission and goals; implementing planning, resource allocation, and institutional renewal processes; using institutional resources efficiently; providing leadership and governance; providing administrative structures and services; demonstrating institutional integrity; and assuring that institutional processes and resources support appropriate learning and other outcomes for its students and graduates. (Standard 7)
Outcomes Assessment	Implementation and subsequent evaluation of the success of the strategic plan and resource allocation support the development and change necessary to improve and to maintain institutional quality. (Standard 2) In the context of the institution's mission, the effective and efficient uses of the institution's resources are analyzed as part of ongoing outcomes assessment. (Standard 3) Assessment of student learning demonstrates that the institution's students have knowledge, skills, and competencies consistent with institutional goals and that students at graduation have achieved appropriate higher education goals. (Standard 14)
Services	The human, financial, technical, physical facilities, and other resources necessary to achieve an institution's mission and goals are available and accessible. (Standard 3)
Instruction	The institution identifies student learning goals and objectives, including knowledge and skills, for its educational offerings. (Standard 11) The institution's curricula are designed so that students acquire and demonstrate college-level proficiency in general education and essential skills, including oral and written communication, scientific and quantitative reasoning, critical analysis and reasoning, technological competency, and information literacy. (Standard 12)

APPENDIX D-2

Regional Accreditation Standards: Provisions Affecting Academic Libraries
(Middle States-2002; effective 2003-04)

ACRL Standards Section	Middle States Association of Colleges and Schools, Commission on Higher Education, Characteristics of Excellence in Higher Education, 2002 edition [Adopted January, 2002; mandatory in 2003-2004]
Resources	The human, financial, technical, physical facilities, and other resources necessary to achieve an institution's mission and goals are available and accessible. (Standard 3)
	In the context of the institution's mission, the effective and efficient uses of the institution's resources are analyzed as part of ongoing outcomes assessment. (Standard 3)
	The institution provides student support services reasonably necessary to enable each student to achieve the institution's goals for students. (Standard 9)
	An institution conducts ongoing planning and resource allocation based on its mission and uses the results of its assessment activities for institutional renewal. (Standard 2)
	In the context of the institution's mission, the effective and efficient uses of the institution's resources are analyzed as part of ongoing outcomes assessment. (Standard 3)
Access	The human, financial, technical, physical facilities, and other resources necessary to achieve an institution's mission and goals are available and accessible. (Standard 3)
Staff	The institution's instructional, research, and service programs are devised, developed, monitored, and supported by qualified professionals. (Standard 10)
Facilities	The human, financial, technical, physical facilities, and other resources necessary to achieve an institution's mission and goals are available and accessible. (Standard 3)
Communication & Cooperation	None Noted
Administration	The institution's administrative structure and services facilitate learning and research/scholarship, foster quality improvement, and support the institution's organization and governance. (Standard 5)
Budget	The human, financial, technical, physical facilities, and other resources necessary to achieve an institution's mission and goals are available and accessible. (Standard 3)

APPENDIX E

Regional Accreditation Standards: Provisions Affecting Academic Libraries
(North Central Association-2002)

ACRL Standards Section	North Central Association, Commission on Institutions of Higher Learning, *Handbook of Accreditation* (2002 Revision)
Planning	"The institution [demonstrates it] has clear and publicly stated purposes consistent with its mission [by] decision-making processes appropriate to its stated mission and purposes." (Criterion 1) "The institution [shows evidence it] can continue to accomplish its purposes and strengthen its educational effectiveness [by providing] plans as well as ongoing, effective planning processes necessary to the institution's continuance." (Criterion 4)
Assessment	"The institution [demonstrates it] has effectively organized the human, financial, and physical resources necessary to accomplish it purposes [by providing] academic resources and equipment (e.g., libraries, electronic services and products, learning resource centers, laboratories and studios, computers) adequate to support the institution's purposes." (Criterion 2)
Outcomes Assessment	"The institution [shows evidence it] can continue to accomplish its purposes and strengthen its educational effectiveness [by] structured assessment processes that are continuous, that involve a variety of institutional constituencies, and that provide meaningful and useful information to the planning processes as well as to students, faculty, and administration." (Criterion 4)
Services	"[The institution] provides its students access to those learning resources and support services requisite for its degree programs." (General Institutional Requirements, no. 18) "The institution [demonstrates it] has effectively organized the human, financial, and physical resources necessary to accomplish it purposes [by] provision of services that afford all admitted students the opportunity to succeed." (Criterion 2)
Instruction	"The institution [demonstrates it] is accomplishing its educational and other purposes [by] assessment of appropriate student academic achievement in all its programs, documenting proficiency in skills and competencies essential for all college-educated adults...." (Criterion 3) "The institution [demonstrates it] has effectively organized the human, financial, and physical resources necessary to accomplish it purposes [by] provision of services that afford all admitted students the opportunity to succeed." (Criterion 2)

APPENDIX E

Regional Accreditation Standards: Provisions Affecting Academic Libraries
(North Central Association-2002)

ACRL Standards Section	North Central Association, Commission on Institutions of Higher Learning, *Handbook of Accreditation* (2002 Revision)
Resources	"[The institution] provides its students access to those learning resources and support services requisite for its degree programs." (General Institutional Requirements, no. 18)
	"The institution [shows evidence it] can accomplish its purposes and strengthen its educational effectiveness [by providing] a current resource base—financial, physical, and human—that positions the institution for the future; [and] resources organized and allocated to support its plans for strengthening both the institution and its programs." (Criterion 4)
	"The institution [demonstrates it] is accomplishing its educational and other purposes [by], if appropriate: evidence of support for the stated commitment to basic and applied research through provision of sufficient human, financial, and physical resources to produce effective research." (Criterion 3)
	"Good practice holds that a basic collection...[is] conveniently available to all of an institution's students (whether on-campus or at other instructional sites)....In addition, institutions should continually enhance their collections of books, bound serials, and other print materials with...newer and often more-convenient forms of information storage and retrieval....Making these resources an integral part of a student's education requires the institution to invest seriously in associated hardware and to provide the staff that can maintain these resources...." (Criterion 2, Special Note on Libraries and Other Learning Resources, p. 37-38)
Access	"[The institution] provides its students access to those learning resources and support services requisite for its degree programs." (General Institutional Requirements, no. 18)
	"[A]ccess to learning resources that contain the world's accumulated and still-developing knowledge is a necessity for students pursuing a higher education....The Commission expects each institution that it accredits to be responsible for assuring that students can and do use the materials essential for their education....Institutions should ensure that their off-campus students have access to adequate learning resources....In addition, institutions should continually enhance their collections of books, bound serials, and other print materials with these newer and often more-convenient forms of information storage and retrieval: microforms, CD-ROMs, audiotape, videotape, CDs, on-line databases, connections to the Internet, and others." (Criterion 2, Special Note on Libraries and Other Learning Resources, p. 37-38)

APPENDIX E

Regional Accreditation Standards: Provisions Affecting Academic Libraries
(North Central Association-2002)

ACRL Standards Section	North Central Association, Commission on Institutions of Higher Learning, *Handbook of Accreditation* (2002 Revision)
Facilities	"The institution has effectively organized the human, financial, and physical resources necessary to accomplish its purposes [by providing] academic resources and equipment (e.g., libraries, electronic services and products, learning resource centers, laboratories and studios, computers) adequate to support the institution's purposes." (Criterion 2) "The institution [demonstrates it] is accomplishing its educational and other purposes [by], if appropriate: evidence of support for the stated commitment to basic and applied research through provision of sufficient human, financial, and physical resources to produce effective research." (Criterion 3)
Communication & Cooperation	None identified.
Administration	"The institution has effectively organized the human, financial, and physical resources necessary to accomplish its purposes." (Criterion 2) "The institution [shows evidence it] can accomplish its purposes and strengthen its educational effectiveness [by providing] a current resource base—financial, physical, and human—that positions the institution for the future; decision-making processes with tested capability of responding effectively to anticipated and unanticipated challenges to the institution; [and] resources organized and allocated to support its plans for strengthening both the institution and its programs." (Criterion 4) "Making [newer forms of information storage and retrieval] an integral part of a student's education requires the institution to invest seriously in associated hardware and to provide the staff that can maintain these resources, train students in their use, and provide assistance when it is needed." (Criterion 2, Special Note on Libraries and Other Learning Resources, p. 37-38)
Budget	"The institution has effectively organized the human, financial, and physical resources necessary to accomplish its purposes [by providing] academic resources and equipment (e.g., libraries, electronic services and products, learning resource centers, laboratories and studios, computers) adequate to support the institution's purposes." (Criterion 2) "The institution [demonstrates it] is accomplishing its educational and other purposes [by], if appropriate: evidence of support for the stated commitment to basic and applied research through provision of sufficient human, financial, and physical resources to produce effective research." (Criterion 3) "The institution [demonstrates] it has effectively organized the human, financial, and physical resources necessary to accomplish its purposes [by] a pattern of financial expenditures that shows the commitment to provide both the environment and the human resources necessary for effective teaching and learning." (Criterion 2)

APPENDIX F

Regional Accreditation Standards: Provisions Affecting Academic Libraries
(New England)

ACRL Standards Section	New England Association of Schools and Colleges, Commission on Institutions of Higher Education, *Standards for Accreditation*, 2001 ed.
Planning	"The institution has a mission and a set of purposes appropriate to higher education, consistent with its charter or other operating authority, and implemented...." (1.1) "Specific objectives, reflective of the institution's overall mission and purposes, are developed for the institution's individual units." (1.3) "Planning and evaluation are systematic, broad-based, interrelated, and appropriate to the institution's circumstances." (2.2) "The institution systematically collects and uses data necessary to support its planning efforts and to enhance institutional effectiveness." (2.3)
Assessment	"The institution evaluates the achievement of its mission and purposes, giving primary focus to the realization of its educational objectives." (2.4) "The institution systematically applies information obtained through its evaluation activities to inform institutional planning, thereby enhancing institutional effectiveness especially as it relates to student achievement." (2.5) "The institution determines the effectiveness of its evaluation activities on an ongoing basis. Results are used to revise and further enhance the institution's implementation of its purposes and objectives." (2.6)
Outcomes Assessment	"To the extent possible, evaluation enables the institution to demonstrate through verifiable means its attainment of purposes and objectives both inside and outside the classroom." (2.4) "The institution ensures that students use library and information resources as an integral part of their education." (7.1) "The institution regularly and systematically evaluates the adequacy and utilization of its library and information resources, and uses the results of the data to improve and increase the effectiveness of these services." (7.6)
Services	"...sufficient collections, information technology systems, and services are readily accessible to students wherever programs are located or however they are delivered. These collections, systems, and services are sufficient in quality, level, diversity, quantity, and currency to support and enrich the institution's academic offerings." (7.2)
Instruction	"The institution provides appropriate orientation and training for use of [library, information resources and services]...as well as instruction in basic information literacy." (7.4)

APPENDIX F

Regional Accreditation Standards: Provisions Affecting Academic Libraries
(New England)

ACRL Standards Section	New England Association of Schools and Colleges, Commission on Institutions of Higher Education, *Standards for Accreditation*, 2001 ed.
Resources	"The institution makes available the library and information resources necessary for the fulfillment of its mission and purposes. These resources support the academic and research program and the intellectual and cultural development of students, faculty, and staff." (7.1) "It allocates resources for scholarly support services compatible with its instructional and research programs and the needs of faculty and students." (7.3) "These collections, systems, and services are sufficient in quality, level, diversity, quantity, and currency to support and enrich the institution's academic offerings." (7.2)
Access	"Through the institution's ownership or guaranteed access, sufficient collections, information technology systems, and services are readily accessible to students wherever programs are located or however they are delivered. These collections, systems, and services are sufficient in quality, level, diversity, quantity, and currency to support and enrich the institution's academic offerings." (7.2) "It provides appropriate support for distance learning students and faculty, such as on-line reference service and contractual access to relevant off-campus library resources." (7.5)
Staff	"Professionally qualified and numerically adequate staff administer the institution's library, information resources and services." (7.4)
Facilities	"The institution provides facilities adequate to house the collections and equipment so as to foster an atmosphere conducive to inquiry, study, and learning among students, faculty, and staff." (7.2) "The institution has sufficient and appropriate physical resources...." (8.1)
Communication & Cooperation	"The institution participates in the exchange of resources and services with other institutions and within networks as necessary to support and supplement its educational programs." (7.5)
Administration	"Clear and disseminated policies govern access, usage, and maintenance of the library, information resources, and services." (7.1) "Through its organizational design and governance structure, the institution creates and sustains an environment that encourages teaching, learning, scholarship, and where appropriate research, and it assures provision of support adequate for the appropriate functioning of each organizational component." (3.1)
Budget	"Institutional decision-making, particularly the allocation of resources, is consistent with planning priorities." (2.3) "The institution provides sufficient and consistent financial support for the effective maintenance and improvement of the institution's library, information resources, and services." (7.3)

APPENDIX G

Regional Accreditation Standards: Provisions Affecting Academic Libraries
(Northwest)

ACRL Standards Section	Northwest Association of Schools and Colleges, Commission on Colleges, *Accreditation Handbook*, 1999 ed.
Planning	"The institution's mission and goals define the institution, including its educational activities, its student body, and its role within the higher education community." (1.A) "The institution engages in ongoing planning to achieve its mission and goals." (1.B) "The primary purpose for library and information resources is to support teaching, learning, and, if applicable, research in ways consistent with, and supportive of, the institution's mission and goals." (5.A) "Library and information resources planning activities support teaching and learning functions by facilitating the research and scholarship of students and faculty." (5.E)
Assessment	"Progress in accomplishing the institution's mission and goals is documented and made public." (1.A.3) "The institution clearly defines its evaluation and planning processes. It develops and implements procedures to evaluate the extent to which it achieves institutional goals." (1.B.1) "The institution has a planning process that involves users, library and information resource staff, faculty, and administrators." (5.E.1)
Outcomes Assessment	"The evaluation proceeds from the institution's own definition of its mission and goals. Such evaluation is to determine the extent to which the mission and goals are achieved...." (1.A) "[The institution] also evaluates how well, and in what ways, it is accomplishing its mission and goals and uses the results for broad-based, continuous planning and evaluation. Through its planning process, the institution asks questions, seeks answers, analyzes itself, and revises its goals, policies, procedures, and resource allocation." (1.B) "Related evaluation processes regularly assess the quality, accessibility, and use of libraries and other information resource repositories and their services to determine the level of effectiveness in support of the educational program." (5.E) "The institution regularly and systematically evaluates the quality, adequacy, and utilization of its library and information resources and services, including those provided through cooperative arrangements, and at all locations where courses, programs, or degrees are offered. The institution uses the results of the evaluations to improve the effectiveness of these resources." (5.E.3)

APPENDIX G

Regional Accreditation Standards: Provisions Affecting Academic Libraries
(Northwest)

ACRL Standards Section	Northwest Association of Schools and Colleges, Commission on Colleges, *Accreditation Handbook*, 1999 ed.
Services	"Adequate library and information resources and services, at the appropriate level for degrees offered, are available to support the intellectual, cultural, and technical development of students enrolled in courses and programs wherever located and however delivered." (5.A) "Information resources and services are determined by the nature of the institution's educational programs and the locations where programs are offered." (5.A.3) "Information resources and services are sufficient in quality, depth, diversity, and currency to support the institution's curricular offerings." (5.B)
Instruction	"Library and information resources and services contribute to developing the ability of students, faculty, and staff to use the resources independently and effectively." (5.B.2)
Resources	"Adequate library and information resources and services, at the appropriate level for degrees offered, are available to support the intellectual, cultural, and technical development of students enrolled in courses and programs wherever located and however delivered." (5.A) "The institution's information resources and services include sufficient holdings, equipment, and personnel in all of its libraries, instructional media and production centers, computer centers, networks, telecommunication facilities, and other repositories of information to accomplish the institution's mission and goals." (5.A.1) "The institution's core collection and related information resources are sufficient to support the curriculum." (5.A.2) Equipment and materials are selected, acquired, organized, and maintained to support the educational program." (5.B.1) "Library and information resources are readily accessible to all students and faculty. These resources and services are sufficient in quality, level, breadth, quantity, and currency to meet the requirements of the educational program." (5.C.1) "The institution provides evidence that it makes available for graduate programs the required resources for faculty, facilities, equipment, laboratories, library and information resources wherever the graduate programs are offered and however delivered." (2.E.1)

APPENDIX G

Regional Accreditation Standards: Provisions Affecting Academic Libraries
(Northwest)

ACRL Standards Section	Northwest Association of Schools and Colleges, Commission on Colleges, *Accreditation Handbook*, 1999 ed.
Access	"Adequate library and information resources and services, at the appropriate level for degrees offered, are available to support the intellectual, cultural, and technical development of students enrolled in courses and programs wherever located and however delivered." (5.A) "Information resources and services are sufficient in quality, depth, diversity, and currency to support the institution's curricular offerings." (5.B) "Computing and communications services are used to extend the boundaries in obtaining information and data from other sources, including regional, national, and international networks." (5.B.5) "The institution provides adequate facilities for library and information resources, equipment, and personnel. These resources, including collections, are readily available for use by the institution's students, faculty, and staff on the primary campus and where required off-campus." (5.C) "Library and information resources are readily accessible to all students and faculty. These resources and services are sufficient in quality, level, breadth, quantity, and currency to meet the requirements of the educational program." (5.C.1)
Staff	"Personnel are adequate in number and in areas of expertise to provide services in the development and use of library and information resources." (5.D) "The institution employs a sufficient number of library and information resources staff to provide assistance to users of the library and to students at other learning resources sites." (5.D.1) "Library and information resources staff include qualified professional and technical support staff, with required specific competencies, whose responsibilities are clearly defined." (5.D.2) "The institution provides opportunities for professional growth for library and information resources professional staff." (5.D. 3)
Facilities	"The institution provides adequate facilities for library and information resources, equipment, and personnel. These resources, including collections, are readily available for use by the institution's students, faculty, and staff on the primary campus and where required off-campus." (5.C)

APPENDIX G

Regional Accreditation Standards: Provisions Affecting Academic Libraries
(Northwest)

ACRL Standards Section	Northwest Association of Schools and Colleges, Commission on Colleges, *Accreditation Handbook*, 1999 ed.
Communication & Cooperation	"The institution uses information from its planning and evaluation processes to communicate evidence of institutional effectiveness to its public." (1.B.9)
	"Opportunities are provided for faculty, staff, and students to participate in the planning and development of the library and information resources and services." (5.B.4)
	"Computing and communications services are used to extend the boundaries in obtaining information and data from other sources, including regional, national, and international networks." (5.B.5)
	"The institution consults library and information resources staff in curriculum development." (5.D.5)
	"The institution, in its planning, recognizes the need for management and technical linkages among information resource bases (e.g., libraries, instructional computing, media production and distribution centers, and telecommunications networks)." (5.E.2)
Administration	"Policies, regulations, and procedures for systematic development and management of information resources, in all formats, are documented, updated, and made available to the institution's constituents." (5.B.3)
	"Library and information resources and services are organized to support the accomplishment of institutional mission and goals. Organizational arrangements recognize the need for service linkage among complementary resource bases (e.g., libraries, computing facilities, instructional media and telecommunication centers)." (5.D.4)
	"The administration and staff are organized to support the teaching and learning environment which results in the achievement of the institution's mission and goals." (6.C)
Budget	"The institution provides sufficient financial support for library and information resources and services, and for their maintenance and security." (5.D.6)
	"Financial planning and budgeting are ongoing, realistic, and based upon the mission and goals of the institution." (7.A)

APPENDIX H-1

Regional Accreditation Standards: Provisions Affecting Academic Libraries (Southern Association-1998; current standards)

ACRL Standards Section	Southern Association of Colleges and Schools, Commission on Colleges, *Criteria for Accreditation.* 1998 edition [applicable through 2003]
Planning	"The statement of purpose serves as the foundation for all institutional operations, programs and activities. Consequently, the institution must demonstrate that its planning and evaluation processes, educational programs, educational support services, financial and physical resources, and administrative processes are adequate and appropriate to fulfill its stated purpose." (Section 3) [page 15; lines 17-24][1] "Each institution must develop a purpose statement for its library and other learning resource services." (5.1.1) [p. 54; 6-8]
Assessment	"[Institutional effectiveness] presumes that each member institution is engaged in an ongoing quest for quality and can demonstrate how well it fulfills its stated purpose." (3) [p. 17; 4-7] "The institution must demonstrate planning and evaluation in its administrative and educational support units." (3.2) [p. 19; 11-12]
Outcomes Assessment	"Each administrative and educational support unit ... must (1) establish a clearly defined purpose which supports the institution's purpose and goals, (2) formulate goals which support the purpose of each unit, (3) develop and implement procedures to evaluate the extent to which these goals are being achieved in the unit, and (4) use the results of the evaluations to improve administrative and educational support services." (3.2) [p. 19; 12-23] "The library and other learning resources must be evaluated regularly and systematically to ensure that they are meeting the needs of users and are supporting the programs and purpose of the institution." (5.1.1) [p. 54; 8-11] "Learning resources and services must be adequate to support the needs of users." (5.1.1) [p. 54; 15-16]
Services	"Each institution must ensure that all students and faculty members have access to a broad range of learning resources to support its purpose and programs, at both primary and distance learning sites. (5.1.2) [p. 54; 26-29] "Priorities for acquiring materials and establishing services must be determined with the needs of the users in mind." (5.1.1) [p. 54; 23-25] "Professional assistance should be available at convenient locations during library hours." (5.1.2) [p. 55; 19-20] "The institution must assign responsibility for providing library/learning resources and services and for ensuring continued access to them at each site. (5.1.7) [p. 57; 31-34] "For distance learning activities, an institution must ensure the provision of and ready access to adequate library/learning resources and services to support the courses, programs and degrees offered." (5.1.7) [p. 57; 23-26]

[1] Section, page, and line number references are from the Eleventh Edition, Second Printing of: Southern Association of Colleges and Schools, Commission on Colleges, Criteria for Accreditation, 1998 edition (Eleventh Edition, Second Printing), Atlanta, 2000.

APPENDIX H-1

Regional Accreditation Standards: Provisions Affecting Academic Libraries
(Southern Association-1998; current standards)

ACRL Standards Section	Southern Association of Colleges and Schools, Commission on Colleges, *Criteria for Accreditation*. 1998 edition [applicable through 2003]
Instruction	"Basic library services must include an orientation program designed to teach new users how to access bibliographic information and other learning resources." (5.1.2) [p. 54; 29-32] "Libraries and learning resource centers must provide students with opportunities to learn how to access information in different formats so that they can continue life-long learning." (5.1.2) [p. 55; 4-7]
Resources	"Institutions must provide access to essential references and specialized program resources for each instructional location." (5.1.3) [p. 56; 1-3] "Priorities for acquiring materials and establishing services must be determined with the needs of the users in mind." (5.1.1) [p. 54; 23-25] "Convenient, effective access to electronic bibliographic databases, whether on-site or remote, must be provided when necessary to support the academic programs." (5.1.2) [p. 55; 26-28] "Institutions offering graduate work must provide library resources substantially beyond those required for baccalaureate programs." (5.1.3) [p. 56; 7-9] "Cooperative agreements with other libraries and agencies should be considered to enhance the resources and services available to an institution's students and faculty members." (5.1.5) [p. 56; 30-33] "The institution must own the library/learning resources, provide access to electronic information available through existing technologies, or provide them through formal agreements." (5.1.7) [p. 57; 26-30]
Access	"Students and faculty must be provided convenient, effective access to library resources needed in their programs." (5.1.2) [p. 55; 23-28] "Access to the library collection must be sufficient to support the educational, research and public service programs of the institution." (5.1.3) [p. 56; 3-5] "Adequate hours must be maintained to ensure accessibility to users." (5.1.2) [p. 55; 17-18] "Library collections must be cataloged and organized in an orderly, easily accessible arrangement following national bibliographic standards and conventions. (5.1.2) [p. 55; 21-23] "Libraries should provide electronic access to materials available within their own system and electronic bibliographic access to materials available elsewhere." (5.1.2) [p. 55; 35-38] "Institutions should supplement their traditional library with access to electronic information." (5.1.4) [p. 56; 21-23]

APPENDIX H-1

Regional Accreditation Standards: Provisions Affecting Academic Libraries
(Southern Association-1998; current standards)

ACRL Standards Section	Southern Association of Colleges and Schools, Commission on Colleges, *Criteria for Accreditation*. 1998 edition [applicable through 2003]
Staff	"Libraries and other learning resources must be adequately staffed by professionals who hold graduate degrees in library science or in related fields such as learning resources or information technology." (5.1.6) [p. 57; 1-4]
	"The number of library support staff members must be adequate". (5.1.6) [p. 57; 14-15]
	"Because professional and technical training in specialized areas is increasingly important in meeting user needs, professionals with specialized non-library degrees may be employed, where appropriate, to supervise these areas." (5.1.6) [p. 57; 9-13]
Facilities	"Libraries and other learning resource centers must have adequate physical facilities to house, service and make library collections easily available; modern equipment in good condition for using print and non-print materials; provision for interlibrary loan services designed to ensure timely delivery of materials; and an efficient and appropriate circulation system." (5.1.2) [p. 55; 29-35]
Communication & Cooperation	"Librarians must work cooperatively with faculty members and other information providers in assisting students to use resource materials effectively." (5.1.2) [p. 55; 7-10]" Librarians, teaching faculty and researchers must share in the development of collections, and the institution must establish policies defining their involvement." (5.1.3) [p. 56; 9-11]
Administration	"Each administrative and educational support unit ... must (1) establish a clearly defined purpose which supports the institution's purpose and goals, (2) formulate goals which support the purpose of each unit, (3) develop and implement procedures to evaluate the extent to which these goals are being achieved in the unit, and (4) use the results of the evaluations to improve administrative and educational support services." (3.2) [p. 19; 12-23]
	"Institutional policies concerning faculty status, salary and contractual security for library personnel must be clearly defined and made known to all personnel at the time of employment." (5.1.6) [p. 57; 18-22]
	"The institution must provide evidence that it is incorporating technological advances into its library and other learning resource operations." (5.1.4) [p. 56; 27-29]
	"Each library or learning resource center must have a policy governing resource material selection and elimination, and should have a procedure providing for the preservation, replacement or removal of deteriorating materials in the collection." (5.1.3) [p. 56; 13-17]
	"Organizational relationships, both external and internal to the library, should be clearly specified." (5.1.6) [p. 57; 17-18]
Budget	"Because the financial resources of an institution influence the quality of its educational program, each institution must possess sufficient financial resources to support all of its programs. (6.3.1) [p.69; [7-10]
	"An institution must prepare an appropriately detailed annual budget. Its preparation and execution must be preceded by sound educational planning." (6.3.3) [p. 70; 11-14]

APPENDIX H-2

Regional Accreditation Standards: Provisions Affecting Academic Libraries (Southern Association-2001; effective 2004)

ACRL Standards Section	Southern Association of Colleges and Schools, Commission on Colleges, Principles of Accreditation: Foundations for Quality Enhancement. [Adopted December, 2001; mandatory after 2003]
Planning	"The institution has a clearly defined and published mission statement specific to the institution and appropriate to an institution of higher education, addressing teaching and learning and, where applicable, research and public service." Core Requirement # 4, p. 8.
Assessment	"The institution has developed an acceptable Quality Enhancement Plan and demonstrates the plan is part of an ongoing planning and evaluation process." Core Requirement # 12, p. 9.
Outcomes Assessment	"The institution engages in ongoing, integrated, and institution-wide research-based planning and evaluation processes that incorporate a systematic review of programs and services that (a) results in continuing improvement and (b) demonstrates that the institution is effectively accomplishing its mission." Core Requirement # 5, p. 8. "The institution identifies expected outcomes for its educational programs and its administrative and educational support services; assesses whether it achieves these outcomes; and provides evidence of improvement based on analysis of those results." Comprehensive Standard (Institutional Mission, Governance, and Effectiveness) # 16, p. 11.
Services	"The institution provides facilities, services, and other learning/information resources that are appropriate to support its teaching, research, and service mission." Comprehensive Standard (Programs) # 25, p. 14. "The institution provides student support programs, services, and activities consistent with its mission that promote student learning and enhance the development of its students." Core Requirement # 10, p. 9. "The institution provides appropriate academic support services." Comprehensive Standard (Programs) # 9, p. 12.
Instruction	"The institution ensures that users have access to regular and timely instruction in the use of the library and other learning/information resources." Comprehensive Standard (Programs) # 26, p. 14.

APPENDIX H-2

Regional Accreditation Standards: Provisions Affecting Academic Libraries
(Southern Association-2001; effective 2004)

ACRL Standards Section	Southern Association of Colleges and Schools, Commission on Colleges, Principles of Accreditation: Foundations for Quality Enhancement. [Adopted December, 2001; mandatory after 2003]
Facilities	"The institution provides facilities, services, and other learning/information resources that are appropriate to support its teaching, research, and service mission." Comprehensive Standard (Programs) # 25, p. 14. "The institution operates and maintains physical facilities, both on and off campus, that are adequate to serve the needs of the institution's educational programs, support services, and mission-related activities." Comprehensive Standard (Resources) # 7, p. 15. "The institution has a sound financial base and demonstrated financial stability, and adequate physical resources to support the mission of the institution and the scope of its programs and services." Core Requirement # 11(a), p. 9.
Communication & Cooperation	None identified.
Administration	"The institution identifies expected outcomes for its educational programs and its administrative and educational support services; assesses whether it achieves these outcomes; and provides evidence of improvement based on analysis of those results." Comprehensive Standard (Institutional Mission, Governance, and Effectiveness) # 16, p. 11.
Budget	"The institution has a sound financial base and demonstrated financial stability, and adequate physical resources to support the mission of the institution and the scope of its programs and services." Core Requirement # 11(a), p. 9.

APPENDIX I

Regional Accreditation Standards: Provisions Affecting Academic Libraries
(Western- Senior Colleges) [1]

ACRL Standards Section	Western Association of Schools & Colleges, Senior College Commission, *WASC Handbook of Accreditation/2001*
Planning	"The institution defines its purposes and establishes educational objectives aligned with its purposes and character." (Standards 1, p. 17) "Planning processes at the institution define and, to the extent possible, align academic, personnel, fiscal, physical, and technological needs with the strategic objectives and priorities of the institution." (4.2, p. 29)
Assessment	"Assessments of the campus environment in support of academic and co-curricular objectives are also undertaken and used, and are incorporated into institutional planning." (4.6, p. 30) "Planning processes are informed by appropriately defined and analyzed quantitative and qualitative data, and include consideration of evidence of educational effectiveness, including student learning." (4.3, p. 29)
Outcomes Assessment	"The institution achieves its institutional purposes and attains its educational objectives through the core functions of teaching and learning, scholarship and creative activity, and support for student learning. It demonstrates that these core functions are performed effectively and that they support one another in the institution's efforts to attain educational effectiveness." (Standard 2, p. 20) "The institution conducts sustained, evidence-based, and participatory discussions about how effectively it is accomplishing its purposes and achieving its educational objectives. These activities inform both institutional planning and systematic evaluations of educational effectiveness. The results of institutional inquiry, research, and data collection are used to establish priorities at different levels of the institution, and to revise institutional purposes, structures, and approaches to teaching, learning, and scholarly work." (Standard 4, p. 29) "The institution employs a deliberate set of quality assurance processes at each level of institutional functioning, including new curriculum and program approval processes, periodic program review, ongoing evaluation, and data collection. These processes involve assessments of effectiveness, track results over time, and use the results of these assessments to revise and improve structures and processes, curricula, and pedagogy." (4.4, p. 30)
Services	"These [information] resources, services and facilities are consistent with the institution's purposes, and are appropriate, sufficient, and sustainable." (3.6, p. 26)

[1] Only the Senior College standards are included here, as the Junior College standards are being revised; a second draft of the proposed new standards is currently under review.

APPENDIX I

Regional Accreditation Standards: Provisions Affecting Academic Libraries
(Western- Senior Colleges) [1]

ACRL Standards Section	Western Association of Schools & Colleges, Senior College Commission, *WASC Handbook of Accreditation*/2001
Instruction	"The institution's academic programs actively involve students in learning, challenge them to achieve high expectations, and provide them with appropriate and ongoing feedback about their performance and how it can be improved." (2.5, p. 21)
Resources	"The Institution holds, or provides access to, information resources sufficient in scope, quality, currency, and kind to support its academic offerings and the scholarship of its members. For on-campus students and students enrolled at a distance, physical and information resources, services, and information technology facilities are sufficient in scope and kind to support and maintain the level and kind of education offered. These resources, services and facilities are consistent with the institution's purposes, and are appropriate, sufficient, and sustainable." (3.6, p. 26)

"The institution's expectations for learning and student attainment are clearly reflected in its academic programs and policies. These include the organization and content of the institution's curricula; admissions and graduation policies; the organization and delivery of advisement; the use of its library and information resources; and (where applicable) experience in the wider learning environment provided by the campus and/or co-curriculum." (2.3, p. 21)

"Student support services—including financial aid, registration, advising, career counseling, computer labs, and library and information services—are designed to meet the needs of the specific types of students the institution serves and the curricula it offers." (2.13, p. 23)

"The institution sustains its operations and supports the achievement of its educational objectives through its investment in human, physical, fiscal, and information resources and through an appropriate and effective set of organizational and decision-making structures." (Standard 3, p. 25) |
| **Access** | "The institution's expectations for learning and student attainment are clearly reflected in its academic programs and policies. These include the organization and content of the institution's curricula; admissions and graduation policies; the organization and delivery of advisement; the use of its library and information resources; and (where applicable) experience in the wider learning environment provided by the campus and/or co-curriculum." (2.3, p. 21)

"Student support services—including financial aid, registration, advising, career counseling, computer labs, and library and information services—are designed to meet the needs of the specific types of students the institution serves and the curricula it offers." (2.13, p. 23)

"The institution holds, or provides access to, information resources sufficient in scope, quality, currency, and kind to support its academic offerings and the scholarship of its members." (3.6, p. 26) |

APPENDIX I

Regional Accreditation Standards: Provisions Affecting Academic Libraries
(Western- Senior Colleges) [1]

ACRL Standards Section	Western Association of Schools & Colleges, Senior College Commission, *WASC Handbook of Accreditation*/2001
Staff	"The institution employs personnel sufficient in number and professional qualifications to maintain its operations and to support its academic programs, consistent with its institutional and educational objectives." (3.1, p. 25)
Facilities	"Fiscal and physical resources are effectively aligned with institutional purposes and educational objectives, and are sufficiently developed to support and maintain the level and kind of educational programs offered both now and for the foreseeable future." (3.5, p. 26) "For on-campus students and students enrolled at a distance, physical and information resources, services, and information technology facilities are sufficient in scope and kind to support and maintain the level and kind of education offered." "These resources, services and facilities are consistent with the institution's purposes, and are appropriate, sufficient, and sustainable." (3.6, p. 26)
Communication & Cooperation	"2.9. The institution recognizes and promotes appropriate linkages among scholarship, teaching, student learning and service." (2.9, p. 22) "The institution periodically engages its multiple constituencies in institutional reflection and planning processes which assess its strategic position; articulate priorities; examine the alignment of its purposes, core functions and resources; and define the future direction of the institution." (4.1, p. 29) "Appropriate stakeholders, including alumni, employers, practitioners, and others defined by the institution, are involved in the assessment of the effectiveness of educational programs." (4.8, p. 30)
Administration	"The institution sustains its operations and supports the achievement of its educational objectives through its investment in human, physical, fiscal, and information resources and through an appropriate and effective set of organizational and decision-making structures. These key resources and organizational structures promote the achievement of institutional purposes and educational objectives and create a high quality environment for learning." (Standard 3, p. 25) "The institution's organizational structures and decision-making processes are clear, consistent with its purposes, and sufficient to support effective decisionmaking." (3.8, p. 27) "Leadership at all levels is committed to improvement based on the results of the processes of inquiry, evaluation and assessment used throughout the institution." (4.6, p. 30)
Budget	"The institution sustains its operations and supports the achievement of its educational objectives through its investment in human, physical, fiscal, and information resources...." (Standard 3, p. 25) "Fiscal and physical resources are effectively aligned with institutional purposes and educational objectives, and are sufficiently developed to support and maintain the level and kind of educational programs offered both now and for the foreseeable future." (3.5, p. 26)